SALES SUCCESS FOR THE SPIRITUAL MINDED SALES PERSON

How to Sell without Losing your Soul

By Steve Lentini

COPYRIGHT 2020 BY STEVE LENTINI

Introduction

Selling from the level of your Soul......is it possible? I say **yes** because I have been successfully selling from the level of my soul for over thirty years. I wanted to be a priest from the early age of five until I met Sophie (that is another story) and thank GOD I did. If she and I did not meet I would have spent the last thirty years celibate.....that's exactly why I did not bother to become a priest, instead my path led me into a career in sales.

Selling from the level of your Soul means that we make a connection to each prospect and customer and we help people buy. If you have integrity and commitment to what you do and a passion for people, then you have what it takes to begin to honor your authentic self, your soul, and people around you will notice the difference.

Gratitude, self respect, boundaries, giving what you want to get are all some of the additional components of Soulful Selling.

We live in a Galaxy, in a Universe, a miracle itself and we can bring this kind of thinking, an unlimited perspective into what we do and created a life of joy, happiness and success.

If you have ever thought about selling and then thought, "well, I am too spiritual for sales", think again. If you are a CEO and thought, "It's best if I leave my spiritual side at home", think again. More and more companies and CEO's are adding spirit to what they do.

Today more than ever, if you are a Universal spirit, a soulful person, you can bring this with you in every moment.

Having a goal, a vision, a dream and then acting toward it is spiritual, except that most people leave behind a set of tools that could propel them beyond anything they could have pictured. In his book, "God is a Salesman"…..by Mark Stevens said…add quote here)

So today, get excited, get ready to succeed with a Universal team on your side and in this book you will read and remember what you already know deep inside.

P.S. your soul is there on every sales call you make and have ever made….how did you feel when your actions did not honor your soul? Honor your soul and watch the Universe unfold to support

STEPHEN LENTINI

your deepest desires.

Acknowledgements

I want to thank all the nay sayers in my life, especially those who I found difficulty dealing with, for being my inspiration to keep writing and doing my soul's work, honoring what is my purpose in this lifetime. All of you were and are truly angel's in my life.

To my wife, Kathyann, my children, Beth, Lisa and Paul, Melissa, Chris and Ashley and my grandchildren, Lacey, Taylor, Lauren and Teagan, Logan, Miles, Harper and little baby boy Haskell on the way… thank you all for being such wonderfully loving people and my source of love and fun.

To my brothers Frank and Stan, who have always loved me unconditionally and some have passed, Seb, Lorraine, David, and Bob… always thinking of you in the next world

To my Mother and Father…..even from the next world, I feel your love and presence.

To my many clients and friends…..I am grateful for all your love and support.

To my webmaster, Drew… thank you, thank you, thank you!

I am grateful for the contribution and love that all you have been to and for me.

Steve

STEPHEN LENTINI

Table of Contents

CHAPTER 1.GRATITUDE

CHAPTER 2. MAKE A CONNECTION, MAKE A SALE

CHAPTER 3. HONOR YOUR SOUL'S WORK

CHAPTER 4.
ADD VALUE

CHAPTER 5.LOVE THE MOMENT

CHAPTER 6. HOW TO SAY "NO" TO A CLIENT

CHAPTER 7. GIVE WHAT YOU WANT TO GET IN EVERY SITUATION

CHAPTER 8. INTEGRITY, WOULD YOU BUY FROM YOURSELF?

CHAPTER 9. VISUALIZATION AND MEDITATION, THE POWER OF THE MIND

CHAPTER 10. SURRENDER AND LEARN TO LIVE IN JOY

PART TWO; THE WHERE THE RUBBER MEETS THE ROAD

Chapter 11. Helping people buy, The new sales methodology

Chapter 12. Be upfront and go for no

Chapter 13. Understand all the people you meet with DiSC
  And how to bond

CHAPTER 14. DETACH FROM OUTCOMES

CHAPTER 15. DEVELOP A SYSTEM TO FOLLOW

CHAPTER 16. SOCIAL MEDIA - GET IT RIGHT

CHAPTER 17. THE SEEDS OF SUCCESS

CHAPTER 18.
THE POWER OF NETWORKING AND HOW TO USE IT.

CHAPTER 19. LOVE BEING BETTER; THINK "THE BEST GETTING BETTER."

CHAPTER 20. REMEMBER: WHAT GOES AROUND, COMES AROUND.

CHAPTER 21. MOTIVATE, MOTIVATE, MOTIVATE THOSE AROUND YOU

CHAPTER 22. DREAM AND BELIEVE IN POSSIBILITIES

CHAPTER 23. STOP THE WHINING AND START WINNING

CHAPTER 24. WE DO LIVE IN A GALAXY, A UNIVERSE

CHAPTER 1.
GRATITUDE

One of my coaches used to say "A grateful heart attracts great things"…….. and practicing this principle for the last ten years has created many wonderful things in my life.

Starting with gratitude for each person and everything each day fills one with wonder and awe for what we mostly take for granted

Keep a journal of what you are grateful for. Write five things that you are grateful for when you wake up and before you go to bed each night or at the least say your gratitude's out loud so that your mind is filled with thoughts of gratitude.

Say things that you are grateful for throughout the day. Tell those around you that you are grateful for the job they perform. When traveling through airports each week, I tell the screeners, "thanks for doing this job, I am grateful"….the response I get is amazing. They say things like, "wow, thank you, we rarely ever hear that"… or "mostly we hear how upset people are or annoyed that we have to check things, thank you"….Their response fills me with even more gratitude as I realize that a grateful heart does attract great things.

Have a call partner each day with which you can share three

things you are grateful for and add things like three daily goals, a reading that inspires you and reminds you that we are spiritual beings having a human experience. You could also add intentions for people around the world and for your family and friends. Make the calls fun and productive.

Practice saying what you are grateful for with family, at the dinner table or in general. You may notice at first that saying what you are grateful for is difficult or you may feel some resistance in your body to the practice…..keep it up no matter what. It is like going to the gym, once you build your gratitude muscle it just gets easier each time. When you first start saying what you are grateful for your brain might respond with thoughts like "your not grateful"……or "your miserable, how could you be grateful"…..over time these thoughts will disappear, especially if you practice dismissing them and as you keep up the practice of saying what you are grateful for, shortly you will see that you actually are a more grateful person.

If you are not able to be grateful for what you have or for all the people in your life, how will you recognize your greater good when it arrives?

Satisfaction is first a choice; feelings follow and being grateful helps that process. Most people in sales are what are known as "A" type personalities. I know that I am or was. I was not happy for exceptionally long because I was always looking for the next thing, person, or event that "would make me happy". The truth that I have learned the hard way is that I will never be satisfied "when" this or that happens, when I make this or that sale or reach this or that goal or have this or that person in my life. Today I make the choice, as often as I remember to be satisfied first and I have discovered that the feelings of being satisfied do just follow those thoughts. Being grateful and thinking about what or who I am grateful for in the morning first thing, throughout the day and before I sleep, helps me maintain the decision that I am satisfied.

Perhaps you are asking now "how does this help my sales career?" Remember that in the Universe there is energy and matter and thoughts are energy. What kind of thoughts does a grateful, satisfied person send out compared to an unsatisfied, ungrateful person? Who would you want to buy from? Have you ever heard someone say, "I am not sure why I like that person, there is just something about them" and have you heard someone say just the opposite? "I am not sure why I do not like that person; there was just something about them"

What do you think that something is? I believe it is the energy of their thoughts. When you are in front of a prospect, send them your blessing silently. Wish them joy, success and happiness....as Deepak Chopra says, "When you go to someone's house for dinner you think to bring a gift, on a business call you can do the same with your good wishes for them."

Read books about gratitude. Study gratitude. Do not just take my word for it, experiment for yourself. There are good books on the topic like Gratitude by Louise Hay and Simple Abundance by Sarah von Bronach and many others. Try what I suggest above for one year and compare the quality of your life before and after your experiment.

Write me or email me with your experiment results and perhaps I will include them in my next book or workshop.

STEPHEN LENTINI

What are you grateful for? Make a List.

CHAPTER 2. MAKE A CONNECTION, MAKE A SALE

In the first moment that you meet someone therein lay a huge opportunity to connect. Make eye contact, match their handshake and smile.

Silently bless them. You could say, "The Divinity in me salutes the Divinity in you, I give you my blessings as a gift" Or you could say "I wish you joy, happiness and success as a gift". You can substitute Divinity with God or the Universal Spirit or with anything positive that you wish.

As I wrote in chapter one, thoughts have power. You are always emitting an energy field with your thoughts. Use them to positively impact your environment. In his book "The Hidden Messages in Water", Masaru Emoto says he discovered that crystals formed in frozen water reveal changes when specific concentrated thoughts are directed toward them. He found that water from clear springs and water that has been exposed to loving words show brilliant, complex, and colorful snowflake patterns. In contrast, polluted water and water exposed to negative thoughts forms incomplete, asymmetrical patterns with dull colors. Use your thoughts to send love, gratitude, and peace into the world and to those around you. How could it hurt?

Take out a pad and take notes. You are there to listen. Pay attention; stay grounded by detaching from outcomes. You are there to help. Leave your attachment to any commission, bonus, and your sales quota at the door. If you are always doing the best you can to help people and to honor your souls' highest purpose, you will be compensated. It is a natural law. You always are getting what you give. On the call, prepare by making a list of questions by doing some research on the company, Buy and read Steve Schiffman's book on questions. Now ask questions. Your primary job is to get information, not to give it. Have questions prepared to help you determine if you are a fit for their needs and vice versa, are they a fit for you? If you honor your soul, you will refuse to do business with someone when your soul is shouting "no, no, not this company, person, etc". How will you know, you may be asking? You will feel it.

Pay attention to how you are feeling. Our bodies have approx. 5 trillion cells......and they are all receptors. Trust that. Our cells are the tools the Universe gave our soul to communicate with our brains. Ego may tell you "make the sale, take the commission" and your soul is screaming no. If you pay attention to how you feel and find a way to say what you are feeling, your integrity will be intact and often time's miracles unfold before our eyes because we honored our higher self.

It could sound something like this "I am feeling uncomfortable, are you?" "What do you think it is?" Often, if you are feeling, your customer or prospect is as well, and they will tell you why. If they respond "no, I am not"......then you need to speak about why you feel uncomfortable, if you do not know in the moment you could say "well, ok, I am not sure either why I feel this way and if something jumps out at me during our meeting I promise to bring it up."

Stay grounded and in touch with what you are feeling through the call. At some point, you do know why you are feeling uncomfortable share it. It could be as follows; "I am feeling uncomfortable because with what you have shared with me so far, I am thinking that we are not a fit for each other, would you like to hear why?" You could also check again with your prospect or customer.... "How are you feeling or are you feeling the same way?"

With male prospects or customers, you could substitute the word sensing for feelings......such as "I am sensing that you are uncomfortable with something" Some men, not all, are not comfortable discussing feelings in a business situation as they are so left brained, especially technically trained or engineering types.

CHAPTER 3. HONOR YOUR SOUL'S WORK

I meet sales people and business people who are working only to pay the bills in jobs that they do not like and worse that do not honor their calling. They do not like the product they sell or the company they work for and yet for the fear of not having enough money to live or fear of what others may think, they delay honoring their purpose. I say delay because eventually the Universe will slide them into the events in life that will bring them to finally honor their soul's calling and it may not be pleasant. They may get fired or laid off and the gift will be the wake-up call to do what they love. If they miss the call, again it is only a delay.

Why wait, why delay?

Leave the job that does not work for you or speak up and change the company that way you risk being fired, and it will be for standing up for what you believe. The Universe always supports those who honor their higher calling. You just must be willing to pay the price.

Olympic athletes pay the price in hours of training and restriction of their social life and they delay of many other goals, in pursuit of their dreams. Most of us are not willing to pay the price and we stuff our desires down in favor of "pay the bills, support the family", etc. I am not saying that these are not worthy things and why not start with small steps to honor your soul's work?

If you love selling and you do not love selling for the company your work for, why not look for work with the company of your dreams? Have you even written your dreams down? Writing your dreams would be the first step then. Honor your soul's desire by getting in touch with exactly what you have always wanted deep down. The word desire means "of the father" translated in Latin. You have come here with your dreams from the Universal pool of energy and matter to manifest those dreams here in this reality. To experience what you have come here with, write it down first.

You may say to me as some have "Steve, I do not even know what I deeply desire or I am not sure that I even have a dream in me".....and to them I say the following;

1. What did other kids come to you for while you were growing up?
2. What did adults expect of you while you were growing up?
3. What things were you good at?
4. What things have surprised you to learn about yourself?
5. Describe to me the times that you realized that hours went by and it felt like just minutes or that you felt like "I was somewhere else".....
6. What do people ask you to do today or what do they ask your advice on?

I also suggest spend time doing what Dr Michael Beckwith calls "visioning"…..it's like a computer downloading images…..get quiet for 15 minutes each morning and evening for a long as it takes……(plan on 90 days and see what happens) and write down the images that come into your mind without questioning them after you complete the 15 minutes. Whatever comes is your souls wish for you.

Another way to clarify what your deepest desires are is to use a method taught by Michael Lossier in his book "The Law of Attraction". What Michael says to do is to write a list of what you DO NOT WANT ANYMORE OF IN YOUR LIFE. So, if it is career that you would like clarity on, write the list……and it could include some of the following.

1. I do not want to work with people who do not respect my ideas.
2. I do not want to work with a company that sells a poor-quality product or does shoddy work.
3. I do not want to work for a leader that is out of integrity.
4. I do not want to work for…..etc, etc, etc.

Once you have completed the list of what you do not want more of, create the list of what you do want more of. So, using the above list it would look like this.

1. I want to work with people who respect my ideas.
2. I want to work for a company that makes a high-quality product and delivers great service; they do what they say they will do.
3. I want to work with a leader whose integrity is high.
4. I want to work with a company that …..Etc, etc, etc.

Writing a purpose statement is also helpful. Below is my purpose statement.

The purpose of my life is to wake people up to the Divine miracle that life is and to wake them up to their souls' purpose so they can create the future that they have imagined.

The beauty of a purpose statement is that you can bring it with you no matter what your work is. Reread my purpose and see if that is true, can I bring that everywhere?

A purpose statement gives you a reason to get up every day. You can go to work even if your job does not yet match your deepest desire. It could be that your day job supports your vision of your dream and helps you pay your way until you can live your dream full time.

CHAPTER 4.
ADD VALUE

Adding value is an idea that Napoleon Hill espoused in his book "Think and Grow Rich". In 1937, when Hill wrote the book, the country was still going through the Great Depression, and it was a time like our adjustment that we went through starting in 2008. What Napoleon Hill theorized was that greed had replaced value in the 1920's and eventually led people and businesses becoming rich without adding anything of value. Conditions such as those described above eventually lead to a collapse or an adjustment period. It happens because value is what people exchange money for.

Hill's premise was that a natural law of the Universe is to give more. One tomato seed, for example, gives in return thousands of seeds. You plant that tomato seed and if the conditions are right, that seed will grow into a tomato plant. That plant will yield many tomatoes, each containing hundreds or even thousands of seeds.

Using that example, we are programmed, like the tomato, to give more naturally It is the desire of our soul to be productive and give without regard for our return. It will come if we do what we came here to do. Do like the tomato does and you will yield many seeds of return.

Dale Carnegie said, "you are always getting what you give". Humans though worry that there is not enough to give more. Many people are concerned more about what they are getting and not able to see that their results in life are related to what they have given out previously.

By focusing on what we are getting we are operating like going to a wood stove and saying give me fire and I will give you wood. There is no fire without giving the wood first. Give your employer more than expected. Give your customers more than expected and you will receive plenty. Many people wonder why their jobs do not fulfill them and it is because they are only giving the least effort and expecting a great return. They are holding back, thinking "when they give me a bonus or a raise, then I will give more." They do not understand the law of compensation. You must first give more to get more. Add value and you will be considered valuable.

Ralph Waldo Emerson wrote a wonderful essay on the Law of Compensation and it is titled "Compensation." Chances are you have had times where you gave more, did you notice how it felt to be generous? If you do not remember, then experiment with it. Give more at work and give more at home. To decide what to give for the experiment, write a list of what you would like to get more of. If it's money, give more money, if it's help, give help, if it's praise and recognition, then praise and recognize those around you, if it's love, give more love, understanding, give more understanding. You get the point by now, give more of what you want to get and see what happens. By experimenting yourself, you get to prove the law will work for you or not. For me, the law works every time without exception. The more I give, the more I get.

CHAPTER 5. LOVE THE MOMENT.

One of the best ways to honor our soul's desires is to stay present in each moment. Like Eckert Tolle says, "there is only now, there is no other moment".

Our souls do not know the past or the future.

New writing 3/21/09

Einstein said "all time is happening now"......

Why do I say to love the moment.....why would it matter?

What about the times that prospects are less than honest or what about the time you worked for a boss who had no integrity or that you knew lied? What about all the uncomfortable moments? All the above are your teachers ......"the Master is within; life is the Teacher".....* Honoring your soul's journey you would have a different perspective on uncomfortable people and challenging times. You would be looking for the gift in each one, knowing that all of life, every moment is Divine.

How would that perspective help you in sales you may be asking?

A person who loves the moment, every moment, would not be defeated at the first no from a potential large client. They would persist. Nothing would be viewed as personal.

A consistent "no" from a large prospect, may be life asking you to learn to persist or asking that you learn to let go of taking yourself or others personally. As far as I can see as I look back on all the uncomfortable events in my life, today I would change not one of them. All of them were gifts, all were valuable teachers for me, helping me to learn and grow and without those moments, I would not be the teacher that I am today. Everything and everyone, especially the uncomfortable ones have been a huge contribution to my life and to all of them and each of them, I owe a debt of gratitude and I am very grateful for and to all of them.

I have learned from rude prospects to challenge them with gentle questions like "you must have just met with a real bad salesperson, it sounds like they upset you"…..in my younger days, I would have just left quickly writing them off. By getting the gift of planting my feet with tough prospects, today they are my best customers. Not all of them mind you, most of them.

I remember the evening that I met Peter Delucca of Spaulding and Sly, a large Boston property management company, now long gone, merged into many other companies….Peter approached me at a BOMA event and said "Well, you're from XXXX Company and we could never buy from you"…….I looked at Peter in the eye and smiled….and said "Hi Peter, (as I looked at his name tag)…..how do you know we would sell you?"…

His response was priceless…..I could see that his spine stiffened…..he pulled back from me in surprise and said….. …. "why would you say that…..most companies are dying to sell us"

I said, "Peter, do you sell everyone?"…. "No" was his reply. I asked him "Why not?"

He said " well, everyone is not a fit for us?" I replied…. "Do you mind if I ask why?"

He said, "well, we are not the least expensive by far and we look for clients that want us to manage full services for them….not piecemeal"……

I said… " well, it's the same for us…..we are the least expensive and we too look for clients who will not pick at us piecemeal".

By standing my firm, Peter learned that we had something in common. That both our companies did not sell everyone, and we were both remarkably successful in the marketplace.

I asked Peter as well… "why did you say you could never buy from us"…..He said, "well, we already have 7 companies like yours that we do business with and we are going to consolidate to one and we have never done business with you….how could we consolidate with you?"

I said, "Peter that makes sense…why wouldn't you want to consolidate with one of the companies that you know and like and already have a track record with…..let's get a drink and enjoy the evening."

I truly meant that. We relaxed together and talked family and other matters and before we moved on to mingle with others I remarked to Peter that I knew about his company and that if, in his consolidation efforts, one of his suppliers tried a maneuver that I was familiar with…..(attempting to keep business at a preferred supplier)…call me I will help you with that……Peter said, "oh what maneuver is it?" I said "Peter, what if one of your present companies mentions it during your work, you won't need me….and if they do not and it does come up…why not call me then….fair enough?"….He said, "ok, you're right….if I need you, I will call….thanks Steve"…..

Well, because I was genuine in my offer to help……and I am sure that he could feel it……wouldn't you know that two weeks later I did get a call from Peter and he did need help with getting around a supplier, Scott Paper at the time, who refused to release his file to other companies that distributed the same brands…..they wanted to help their big customer in the Boston market retain the business.

I said to Peter…. "before you tell me what is happening, let me tell you"….I proceeded to tell him what I had seen Scott Paper attempt before…..and Peter replied…. "yes Steve, that's it, your right….that is what they are trying to do….block my consolidation efforts"……so I said "do you like that supplier?"….he said "no"….. "they are one of the suppliers that we have already decided not to award the consolidation to"…..I said "I do not mind helping you at all, would mind doing me a favor?"…..What do you think Peter replied to my request. "No Steve, I don't mind at all, what is it?"….I asked him "would you mind putting me on that list of suppliers that you are considering consolidating to?"

He said… "Steve, not a problem, you are on the list, now tell me what I do?"

I told him and my solution worked like a charm….all of his pricing was released to all the Scott distributors in the Boston marketplace.

So, a day later, Peter faxed me his list of supplies. I looked it over and called Peter back.

"Peter, hi, this is Steve...I got your list and I have a problem"......He said "oh, what is the problem".....I said, "well, we cannot participate in your consolidation efforts...I am sorry".....he said, "why Steve"....shocked....I could hear it....and disappointed....I said... "well, with the number of suppliers that you have, you will not get the best volume considerations from the manufacturers unless you are willing to move from 7 Paper lines to say 3 and 8 trash liner suppliers to say 3....can you see how you could move volume up with fewer manufacturers?".....Peter thought a moment... "Steve, would you recommend what we should do and fax it back to me......and would you suggest the way that would help you stay in the running?"

I said "Sure, yes, I'll be glad to make recommendations, and you make the final call of course".

I faxed him back MY SUGGESTED list of suppliers....all of whom I had good relations with and had in stock....and guess what list Peter re-faxed to all the distributors under consideration? That's right...mine.......He removed our name from the letter and cut and pasted his letterhead on my list......and mind you...it was a good idea....he did get better pricing by showing fewer manufacturers a large increase in volume.

Guess who was awarded the contract.

One week later....for a total of four weeks after we met at that cocktail party......Peter called me to say... "Steve, would you come to my office".......I said sure...... "what will be on the agenda?"....Peter replied.... Well, you are not the lowest cost distributor.....and I'd like to talk about that..." I replied... "Peter, I cannot move any lower...I am sorry"......he replied... "would you come in on Tuesday"......I said, "ok sure and for?"

He said, "I am going to award you the business and I want to talk about getting started".

The miracle of this sale was amazing and all due to my willingness to be honest and tell Peter all along the way what did not work for me. I was never attached to the sale, only in the moment, telling him the truth about what worked or not for our company. That sale was over $700,000 annually and Peter and I met once face to face until we met a second time to go over the award....all the rest was phone and fax. Stay in the moment. Pay attention to what is the highest integrity for your company and state it. Be willing to walk away sales that do not fit and be willing to help customers with the best solutions, even if it means help them get the best deal with their existing suppliers, if they aren't going to switch anyway......by helping them you gain a reputation as someone who is of the highest integrity and you will never have to be the "least expensive" provider.

CHAPTER 6. HOW TO SAY "NO" TO A CLIENT

This chapter's inspiration comes from a book that I love and recommend for every sales person, on a spiritual path or not. Written by William Ury, he talks about the power of knowing "what you are saying yes to in yourself, when you are saying no".

Many sales people, many good sales people in fact, are people pleasers. The love to say yes to clients and prospects, which means, often they over promise and they set the company to under deliver.

To help people pleasers say no....William Ury takes his readers through an exercise that defines boundaries.....what are they saying yes to in themselves when they have to say no?"

For example.....if you say no to a two week delivery on software installation because you know your company is taking six weeks.....you would be saying yes to reducing the stress of all the customers calls that get angrier and angrier as you miss the deadline that you promised because you thought you would lose the sale if you said no.

Ury also points out ....how to say no.... it would sound like this "well, I can definitely say yes to 8 weeks and know you will be satisfied....what is your experience with other software companies?"…let them answer….then you could say… "would you risk giving the contract to another company that promises two week installation based on what you know about most software companies….?" Again, let them answer……then you could ask " would it be worth it to wait the 8 weeks knowing that we told you the truth and most likely, in my experience, that is what most software companies would require if not more time?"…..

I have consulted with software companies and I know that 90% of them are known for missing promised deadlines and promised pricing on contract work. If you tell the truth, would you really want to do business with a company that would not want to hear and accept the truth. I say to clients, "if the truth does not sell, don't sell it"…….walk away.

Being willing to walk away means that you have faith that you could not lose what is yours by Divine Inspiration.

CHAPTER 7 GIVE WHAT YOU WANT TO GET IN EVERY SITUATION

Dale Carnegie once said "you are always getting what you are giving. This is one of the Universal Laws. The Universe responds to like with like, Cause and Effect. What you give out comes back like a boomerang. That being the case, in every situation, before you make a choice about what action to take, ask yourself, what would I want to get back here? In one year, in three, in five and in ten years.

Keep giving what you want to get back no matter what and without regard for where it will come back or from whom.

Do not give to someone and expect that what you give will come back from that person, just know that like gravity, the law works every time, all the time without exception. We cannot see gravity and yet it works, and we trust that it does because we have physical evidence of it. If you look at your life and take responsibility for creating everything that came to you because of what you have given out in the past, you too will see evidence that giving causes getting.

Experiment for yourself. Test it. If you want more understanding, become more understanding. If would want more money, give more money. If you want happier, joyous people in your life, become happier and more joyous yourself every day and watch what happens.

I have conducted this experiment with my own life for over the last ten years and I can say for me, without exception that this law has worked for me.

Conduct research on tithing. Many of the world's richest people have given a tithe of 10% of their income or more to their source of spiritual support. John D Rockefeller started tithing $9.00 per month on his $90.00 income and the total he tithed over his life time was reported to be over $500,000,000.....that's Five Hundred million dollars.....from the late 1800's until the early 1900's.....imagine how much money that is in today's dollars.....he tithed billions of dollars by today's value of the dollar.

Do the research. Experiment and prove it to yourself.

CHAPTER 8. INTEGRITY, WOULD YOU BUY FROM YOURSELF?

Having Integrity and taking a stand for integrity is another key to Soulful Selling. If you are out of integrity or working for a company that is out of integrity, you will pay the price for it. Your results will reflect it and your customers will mirror that action back to you. You will be surrounded with clients that take actions that are out of integrity with you. Remember, you give what you give in a cause and effect world.

"If you have integrity, nothing else matters.

If you do not have integrity, nothing else matters."

Author Unknown

"Do what you say you will do. Keep your word, no matter what the pain, do it." Steve Lentini

Have you ever heard the expression, "My word is my bond?" How many people have you met or live or work with now, do not keep their word and yet they walk around thinking their word is their bond?

Lawyers write page upon page of contract for businesses. Most will not conduct business on their word. Our word as a society as lost its value. Even with signed contracts there are record numbers of court cases today disputing what is written.

Twenty-seven years ago, I sold my company without a contract, on a handshake and a man's word and he kept every bit of it. Gerry Baum, President of Eastern Bag and Paper Co., in Connecticut. I will never forget him or that he kept his word.

My mother kept her word to the creditors of a restaurant that my father owned. In 1957 or 58, they closed the restaurant and owed over $50,000 to creditors. My father took a job with the State of Connecticut as a chef at the Connecticut Valley Hospital, in Middletown, Ct. With debt over ten times what my father made (about $5,000 per year at the time), my mother vowed to pay everyone, and it took many years and she did. She kept her word no matter what. She could have filed for bankruptcy and with seven children, I think the judge back then might even have agreed with that action......and no, she gave her word.

If you work for a company that does not keep its word, challenge them, or quit. Either way you will be amazed at the result. I took a stand once against the President of a company that I worked for on 2006 because he wanted us to break our word and not pay a client who had earned a rebate of $13,000+ and I told him and my direct boss that it did not work for me to break our word. I remember the President saying to me "But I did not give my word we would pay him"......I replied, "yes buy I did and so did Cheri (she was my boss)". He was saying that our integrity as a company was worth less than $13,000+ because he was willing to break it for that amount. He said to me "why are you fighting for this client who left us"......I said, "I'm fighting for our integrity because we gave our word".

After six weeks of discussion, he agreed, and we paid the check although many people told me that he personally put a target on my back.

I did not care because all my life I have had many jobs offers, clients, and a steady stream of income from multiple sources because I have followed these principles. Not perfectly mind you, but when I realized that something was out of whack, I fixed it. With an apology, or a check or whatever it took to make it right. Two years later, I was approached by that company that I stood up for and got the $13,000+ check with a job offer that almost doubled my income from the previous job and what do you think they mentioned when we negotiated about the Director of Sales position? They immediately thanked me for standing up for them and said, "we know the kind of person you are and what you stand for......thank you for standing up for us". They also said, "We did not want you to risk your job for us"........I said, "Don't worry, I didn't, I wouldn't work for a company that did not have integrity, if they had not paid the check, I would have left anyway."

Being in Integrity does not mean you have to be perfect; life is about learning from our mistakes, just clean up your mess once you realize you made it.

You have nothing to fear from anyone who would ask you to compromise your Integrity. I ended up working for the company I stood up for and I did not see that coming until it came and I certainly did not see it in 2006 when I stood up for what was right.

Trust in the cause and effect Law of Attraction and you will see that what you give, you are always getting.

STEPHEN LENTINI

Write about integrity, have you broken you word? How did that make you feel? When you keep your word, how do you feel? What impression does either leave with people?

9. Visualization and Meditation, the power of the mind

"The greater danger for most of us is not
that our aim is too high, and we miss it,
but that it is too low, and we reach it."
- Michelangelo

"Imagination has power" Einstein

If we get still and sit quietly, noticing our thoughts and feelings, our deepest desires do speak to us. The longing of our soul comes through. Dare to aim high, listen to the longings. Honor them by seeing them, visualizing, and feel what it would feel like to achieve them. Picturing what you want has power. Tiger Woods plays a complete round of golf in his mind before playing any tournament. After he walks the course and gets an idea of how he would play each hole, he then visualizes playing each hole. Jack Nicholas used to picture each shot in his mind before each swing. Think about their level of play. When I first heard about the power of visualization, I was skeptical. So, I decided to test it, with things that were a big stretch, so big, that I knew if they did come true, would be definite proof that visualization worked. I pictured in my mind almost every morning before rising and each evening before sleeping both events. I followed the instructions from the book "How to have what you want and want what you have" by John Grey, the Author of Men are from Mars and Women are from Venus. Within 90 days the first event happened. I had been picturing being paid upfront for $25,000 of consulting. If you know the consulting field, mostly you are paid as you deliver the work and sometimes a lot later. I started the visualization in September and in January I had a conversation with a client that I had just completed a three-month sales training program.

"Hi Mark, Steve......Happy New Year and thank you for your business last year"

"Hi Steve, you are welcome" said Mark.

"Mark, for the New Year, I am looking for companies that would like help with managing their sales team, if your customers mention that they need some help, would you mind referring me?"

Mark's clients were all in the Distribution business and they all had sales teams.

Mark said, "well Steve, I was actually thinking of asking you to coach me on managing the team every Monday.....what would you charge me to come in every Monday for six months?

I said "$30,000 and I would like to be paid upfront" to that Mark replied, "What kind of discount do I get for paying you upfront?"

I replied..... "Mark, if you pay me upfront, I'll give you a $5000.00 discount."

Mark replied, "are you in the neighborhood?" I said "sure".......he said stop by if it's not a problem getting $12,500 today and $12,500 in two weeks".

Well, how fast do you think I dropped by?

And I had just manifested the first part of my visualization experiment.

When I called him, I had no idea that this conversation would unfold. I was just following the plan that I had laid out before the New Year to call certain clients to ask for referrals. I was not even thinking of Mark as a potential for my sales management consulting. I followed the prompting to make a list of people to call for referrals and Mark's name was on the list.

In June, I had a credit line of $20,000, the second event that I was visualizing; another thing that I thought for sure would prove the power of picturing to me. I was convinced.

A credit line is virtually unheard of for a training business that was only a year old and had no assets. The only trainer was me and I had a desk, chair and a phone and my office was in my home. I could not use the home for leverage as it was newly purchased and in my wife's name (she would not sign, and I did not ask her). What really cemented this proof in my mind was that it was a *client* that personally co-signed for me when he heard that a credit line would really help my business!

Imagine, most relatives would not sign for a loan, and here a client signed for me.

My process was to picture each morning and evening as I mentioned above and the specific instructions included, "see the client contract, see the amounts that you want, see the hand shake and the signed contracts, see the check, and feel what it feels like to get the check".

With the credit line I did the same thing, I even saw in my mind, the signed loan agreement, (I saw my signature only) and the check and felt what it would feel like having it.

Believe me, when driving home from each event, it felt greater than I had imagined because I was shaking with excitement over what I was going to visualize thereafter.

I visualized a second location to train from, a business partner and more and they all came true.

Imagine what I am picturing now?

Oh wait; no…..spend the time imagining what you desire. Prove it to yourself.

Write it down, do it now…..write out your dream and picture it!

10. Surrender and learn to live in Joy

When you are frustrated, feeling stuck, depressed, or feeling like you have failed, let it go, surrender to the moment. I believe that we are all one with this energy called a Universe, and whatever created this wondrous miracle, we are one with that. "The Master is Within; Life is the Teacher". When you feel stuck, etc, life is either asking you to persist, learn a lesson or get out of the way. There is power in surrender. Men have difficulty not working to fix what is broken. Let it go.

On November 13th, 2002, I was conducting a sales seminar one second and in the next second, I needed an ambulance. Rushed off to the emergency, I remember thinking and saying to the EMT's that I was grateful for whatever I had and the events unfolding as I knew it was going to change my life forever.

Well, I got to the emergency room in a small hospital in Waltham, Massachusetts, (now closed)......and there a 100 day journey began and little did I know I would be out of work six months, but the crossroads moment came five days later.

It was a Wednesday, I arrived around 4:30pm, by midnight on Thursday, and I was in intensive care......and getting progressively worse. I do not remember the Doctor mentioning my diagnosis, and I do remember him saying "You should plan on a long stay"......I thought "Well most stays are three or four days, so what is long a week....ten days?"

By Monday, my body was fighting the effects of Acute Necrotizing Pancreatitis by retaining fluid to protect my internal organs from all the digestive enzymes that had burst from my pancreas into my body cavity. I had gained over 25 pounds of fluid. By retaining fluid, my heart was also surrounded by fluid and I was in danger of congestive heart failure.

And then it happened. I remember two friends sitting at the end of my bed, Warren, and Janice, one second and the next second I was in a large room.

There were people I recognized and there was someone speaking at the front of the room. I remember thinking, "someone is speaking, let me move closer to hear what he is saying"......as I thought that, I moved. I realized that it was a eulogy and I remember thinking "this person has touched a lot of live, let me move closer" and again I moved. As I did, I realized that it was my eulogy and that I had touched a lot of live......in that next second I was asked a question "stay or go". It was a gently voice, very loving, there was no sadness, just peace.....I remember thinking, "well, I have touched a lot of lives, thy will be done".....and I totally surrendered to what was next.

What was next? I was back in the hospital room with Warren and Janice.

I did not mention that event to Warren and Janice for a few weeks and when I did, then know when it was....they knew it was Monday the 18th of November and I asked how they knew.....Warren said, "well, the doctor came in at that moment, you were out of it and said you had better call his family this is it".

What I learned is that you do take something with you when you die, the lives you touch. All the rest does not matter. There was no mention of all the "things" I had owned or the jobs and titles I had or the money I made......and no mention of the mistakes I had made either.....only the lives I had touched.

My total surrender to whatever was next taught me a few things.

1. The only thing that matter in this life, are the lives we touch
2. We can take that with us
3. There is nothing, no one to fear…….nothing…..live fearlessly in the moment, speaking your truth and following your soul's desire.
4. We are here to learn, to grow, to make mistakes. Religion has us fearing a bitter, revengeful, punishing GOD……it is not true, and I experienced it firsthand. We are here to make those mistakes and learn from them. To learn to apologize, to learn to forgive, to learn period. The perfect, sin free life is not one of growth and it is unrealistic. We are not perfect, and we can learn to help each other without fear of loss. There is no loss in a Universe. I had consciousness on both sides, simply different.

What I tell people from my experience is to follow their soul's desire. Go for your biggest, grandest vision of your "self". That is what we are here to do.

I love every moment and I love the opportunities to help people along the way, to touch a life with my message and with whatever I can do to help.

Now back in my body, I do note it is more challenging to surrender, I must remind myself to do it and that all is ok no matter what. Each time I do surrender to the moment (after all it is already here) …. A miracle occurs. When I sense frustration, I let go and something new unfolds. Sometimes the phone rings with help, or an answer. Sometimes, its a few days or weeks or months and I see the reason for what I was feeling frustrated about when it happened. But each time I do surrender to the moment, my life gets better. I am reminded that I do not have to struggle, but to dream and pay attention to life's prompts to act. I take that action……when I am prompted. Those prompts are my intuition. The more I use my intuition, trust it, and follow it, the better. Many people call intuition "following my gut"……whatever you call it, trust it, relax, surrender to what is happening in the moment. You will be amazed at how much better your life works.

Write about "prompts" that you have followed that worked and write about the times you did not follow a "prompt or gut feeling" and what happened.

CHAPTER 11. HELPING PEOPLE BUY, THE NEW SALES METHODOLOGY

Helping people buy is updated way of selling. No pushing to get the sale, no "tacky tactics", instead develop a curiosity for "what is troubling your prospect." Ask yourself, "How can I best help this company or this person?" Be authentic and detach from any ideas of "closing this prospect" and instead be their to genuinely help them find the best solutions or products, even if you hear that some other solution, some other company or product would be better suited for them. Think Infinite Game as Simon Sinek says… not finite like a score of "I win, and they lose."

Helping people buy fits in perfectly for anyone who recognizes the power in doing good, doing the right thing for everyone they meet. Wonder ahead of the meeting and during "is this client the best fit for what I sell, will it be the best solution for them." Ask questions that help them hear if you are a fit or not. Prepare a list of "what you can say yes to" and ask your client ahead of time to do the same. It would sound like this; "Before we meet, would you write down what would work for you as a solution (or product) and what you could say yes to? My goal is to find you the best possible outcome even if it is not me or my company. We do have great companies that we refer our clients to if what we have is ultimately not the best fit? 'Would you mind doing that and sharing it with me after I share what is our best fit?"

Do you hear the difference between this approach and the typical approach of "telling someone how great you and or your company is?"

Below are two stories that demonstrate my point.

Some stories of success.

My best and most memorable sales started at "no"

1. Harvard University

How this happened was my ability to detach from outcomes and be fully present with future clients. It was a natural skill and at the time it was not taught...I thought for sure if anyone found out I did this...I would have been fired...and look what happened in two instances...

> My best and most memorable sales started at no. I remember as I write this my first call with a sales rep that worked for me at Harvard University. The buyer, Linda, started our appointment with "We could never buy from you" ....I said, "Oh, I'm a little confused then, why did we get the appointment" ....

> I was very confused at that moment, wouldn't you be? I like to pay attention to what I am feeling and what I notice about the buyer's body language or facial expressions. I then find a way to say what I am feeling or noticing.

> Linda replied to my question. "Oh, we heard a lot about your company and since you're new to Massachusetts, I figured we would find out about you."

> I replied, "Oh, what did you hear"? She told me. I then

asked "Linda, since we are not going to get the business, would you mind telling me all about what you are looking for and why we cannot get the business."

Linda replied "We currently have 16 suppliers and with some we have done business for over 30 years...so you see we could never give the business to you, we have never even done any business and we are going to select one supplier from the sixteen and consolidate all of our purchases.

I said, "That makes sense...it's probably what I would do" ... "Would you mind telling me about your process of selection and what you are looking for the finalist to do for you?

She replied, "sure, no problem..."

Linda went on to tell me all about her process, what she was looking for her selected supplier to give her, etc..... over 45 minutes talking with someone who told me that we did not have a chance.

I ended our call with "you know Linda, it sounds to me like you're looking for a supplier partner" and she replied, "oh, partnership, what do you mean, would you explain that." I replied, "well, aren't all of your suppliers going to be coming into your review and selection process" Linda replied "yes" .... I said, "why don't you wait and see if your current suppliers have the same idea and if not, call me I'll be glad to share it with you." She agreed that was fair.

Two weeks later, I got a phone call from Linda at Harvard, asking me to come in and explain my vision of a supplier partner. I said, "sure Linda, would you do me a favour?" She replied, "no problem, of course." I said, "would you mind putting me on that list of suppliers that you are considering?"

She said "yes." I was on cloud nine that day.

Six months later, after a complete review of all the suppliers, and a bunch of work by a great team of people, WE GOT THE BUSINESS. THE COMPANY THAT LINDA SAID, "NO, WE COULD NEVER BUY FROM YOU"....

We were awarded the contract for over $1 million dollars in annual sales....!!!!

2. Spaulding and Slye.

Six months later...I met Peter of Spaulding and Slye Real Estate management at a BOMA cocktail party and he saw my name badge and said "oh, you're with XXXX Paper company, we could never buy from you"'... and I said to Peter, "how do you know that I would sell you"....

He was a little stunned and said, "why wouldn't you sell us"? I asked him, "Do you sell everyone in your market" ... he replied "no." I said, "why not?" Peter replied "well, not everyone is a fit..." and I asked "and that is because" ...Peter replied "well, we cannot make money on every situation so we have to find out if we are a fit" ...

I said to Peter, "Well it the same for us" ...he understood. We spoke the rest of the evening and exchanged cards. I asked him before we parted, "how come you said that you could never buy from us...he said "oh, we have six or seven paper companies now and I am going to consolidate them to one and we have never even purchased from you"....

Well, there is a lot more to the story and guess what happened a few weeks later? That is right, I got the business... over $750,000 annually...

What is more...when I got to Boston one year earlier, I said to those around me "I am going to get Harvard and Spaulding & Slye" ...

Funny how things work out...

Great things start at "no." It takes the pressure off everyone. You can say what is important and the truth.

I say go for no in your conversations with Prospects. You cannot lose what you do not have anyway.

Go get a no 20 times today and 100 for the month and see what happens.

What occurred in both stories was that I offered to help both future customers have their opinion which started out as "We could never buy from you.." and although they each were somewhat different they both began at a similar point. I did not push back like typical salespeople, instead I let them have their space and them asked "Ok, why... tell me about how you came to that conclusion...?"

I detached from the outcomes and *wanted to help them.* That is how I approached all prospects... "how could I help them even if I was not going to get the sale?" Look at the result in both cases. When I tell those stories to salespeople today, they are amazed at the miracle that occurred... **they both came back to me!**

People can feel your energy and the energy of detaching

from outcomes and authentically wanting to help people find the best outcome is attractive because it relieves the prospect of what they feel from a pushy sales person who is only concerned with their commission. I call that "commission breath" and it stinks.

The energy of authentically wanting to do the best for people even if it is not you is an attracting force. As you can see from both stories, they came back to me for the help I offered, and it resulted in miraculous outcomes.

CHAPTER 12: BE UPFRONT AND GO FOR NO

How many salespeople are comfortable going for *no*? We worry about rejection. We cannot relax. Starting at *no* is more fun and it takes the pressure off both of you.

Instead of going for *no* early, we let the customer have control of the sale and we waste time and resources in calls that are going nowhere. We wait and wonder if the customer finds value in what we say.

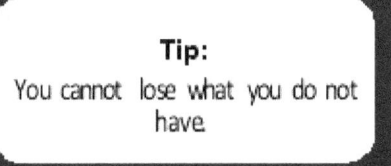

Tip:
You cannot lose what you do not have.

Let me suggest a different approach. Give your customer/prospects the opportunity to say *no* and watch what happens. I guarantee that 70 - 80% of the time that the real dialogue will begin after the first *no*.

Here is an example of giving your customer or prospect the opportunity to say *no* –

"Thank you Mr. / MS. Prospect for inviting me in. I have prepared an agenda for our time together. Do you mind if I review it? I am going to ask you some questions about your company and then you can ask me about mine. If after our exchange you **cannot** see a reason for our two companies to get together **for now, for this moment**, would you mind sharing that with me? I am okay with it. If, on the other hand, you do see a reason to move forward, would you let me know that as well? Then together we can determine what the next step will be. Are you okay with that?"

Giving your prospect the opportunity to say *no* is refreshing. A salesperson who is trying to take the pressure off them will surprise them.

If they say *no*, ask them why? Listen carefully. Your true selling starts here. **TIP:** No is a sales person's friend at no, go with it and find the

GOLD!

For example, if after your questions you ask, "Well Mr. /Ms. Prospect, have you heard or seen any reason for me to continue?" If they respond, "no", now ask, "May I ask why?" Let's suppose the prospect responds', "Well, I'm happy with my current supplier and I'm not going to change." You could respond, "I appreciate that; under what circumstances would you consider a change?" **Listen** - or you might say, "I hear that you are happy with your current supplier, however, no one is perfect. In fact, we are not; but if you had a magic wand, what, if anything, would you improve about your current supplier?"

Do you see what I am saying? Even after you get a *no*, you have established dialogue after the *no*, with questions. It's the dialogue you want. Look for openings in their answers to your questions - listen carefully.

If it is no, you have shortened the selling cycle, and now you can move on to more prospects sooner. Remember to remind them that *no* was for now. Ask if they mind if you return from time to time if you have an idea or suggestion for them. Ask them what kind of ideas or suggestions would they appreciate? What areas of their business are they looking for ideas to improve?

They will respect your approach and invite you back.

Whatever your concerns are, come up with a question that deals with the issue up front and wait for the answer. You will never need a "tacky tactic" if you say what you are feeling. Find a way to say it. If you feel uncomfortable about bringing something up, say that you feel uncomfortable about something and you wondered if you could bring up something that they might find uncomfortable.

Whatever your fears are, find a way to bring them up as well. If someone asks for your pricing early in the sales call, you might fear that they are just shopping to compare and give your pricing to their current supplier. If you feel that, you would say, "My biggest fear is that if I give you a price list now, you will bring it to your current supplier just to lower your pricing. I have had that happen before. Could it be the reason you are asking for pricing just now?"

Remember my acronym for FEAR: **F**acing "**E**normous" **Ad**versity **R**ealistically/**R**esponsibly.

When we feel fear, it is an indicator from our body that some action is required on our part. Face it. Walk into it. I put the word

"Enormous" in quotes because often when we fear something, we have made it enormous. When we get to the other side of the issue, we look back and think, "Why did I fear that? It was not a big deal after all". I say realistically/responsibly as some situations call for common sense. If your personal safety is involved for example, *realistically* would mean get out of there. *Responsibly* would mean to be sure that our response is with integrity, that we do the right thing.

Facing "enormous" adversity realistically/responsibly

If you notice that something you said may have upset the prospect, bring it up. You could say, I am feeling like I have said something that upset you, is that the case?

If the prospect says something that confuses you or says something

that you are curious about, find a way to say it.

This is called the "Pendulum Theory of Communication", to have an adult-adult conversation, your goal is to always stay farther on the negative (Not OK) than the positive (OK).

Most prospects will be refreshed with your honesty and find a way to help you keep the sale.

There is nothing to remember in this selling method, just be yourself, be honest and if you feel it, use that.

In communication, your goal is always to have an adult-adult conversation. That is achieved by always saying what you feel. Soften with soft people and hit the tough people with it hard, mirroring each of them. Tough people like and respect tough people. The same goes for softer style folks. Just mirror them. Look at the diagram below:

Look at each position on the pendulum on the page 48;

12: No/Never buy, abrupt.

11: Takes phone calls when you are there, obnoxious,

Do not want you here, rude

10: Defending competition

9: Shuts you off

8: Fidgeting, inattentive, and occasionally listening

7: Uncomfortable

6: Neutral

5: Maybe, head nods, wishy-washy

4: Sounds good

3: Likes you

2: Enthusiastic

1: Sold/Yes

Wherever your prospect is on the pendulum, you stay on the negative side. If they are sold, #1, you drop down to #4, by saying "Sounds good, tell me what you mean by "wow, I've been wanting to get that from you?" A good many sold or enthusiastic prospects either have no money or no intention of ever

buying. They are people pleasers who cannot say "no" to your face. These are the people that you chase with voice mails, after they tell you, "Oh, yes, I'll get it on Monday, just call me then". On the other end of the scale, say at #12, they say, "No not today, not ever from your company", you would say, "You sound upset with us, what happened, tell me about it?" You would also be saying what you feel at this moment. Instead of defending your company, be empathetic and be curious about what happened. Give the upset person the space for their feelings and let them vent. Do not apologize until you have heard the whole story. Agree with them if you can, say, "Well, I'm not sure that I would buy from us after that." There is no guarantee that they will ever buy, but I have had some of the best sales in my life after a prospect or customer started with how angry they were with us and with "No, we'll never buy from you."

Be aware of where people start out on the pendulum of communication. Remember, your job in any sales conversation, especially if you have just met the prospect, is to stay below them, you stay "less ok" than they are if they are on the positive. And on the negative side, you would carefully mirror their negative, and use what I call a takeaway. I once had a prospect come up to me at a cocktail reception and say "Oh, you're with XXXX, we could never buy from you." and I replied, "How do you know that we would sell you?"

He was shocked that I might not want to sell them. I could see by his reaction. His spine stiffened. He asked, "How come you might not sell us?" I asked him, "Do you sell everyone?" He replied, "No." I asked, "Peter, (looking at his name badge) why not?" Peter replied, "Well, not everyone is a good prospect for us." I said, "Well, the reason we might not sell you is the same. You might not be a good fit for us. Tell me a little bit about why you said you would never buy from us." -- and that started a dialogue that ended with me closing his business a few weeks later; it was worth over $750,000 annually. Why did I gain

SALES SUCCESS FOR THE SPIRITUAL SALESPERSON

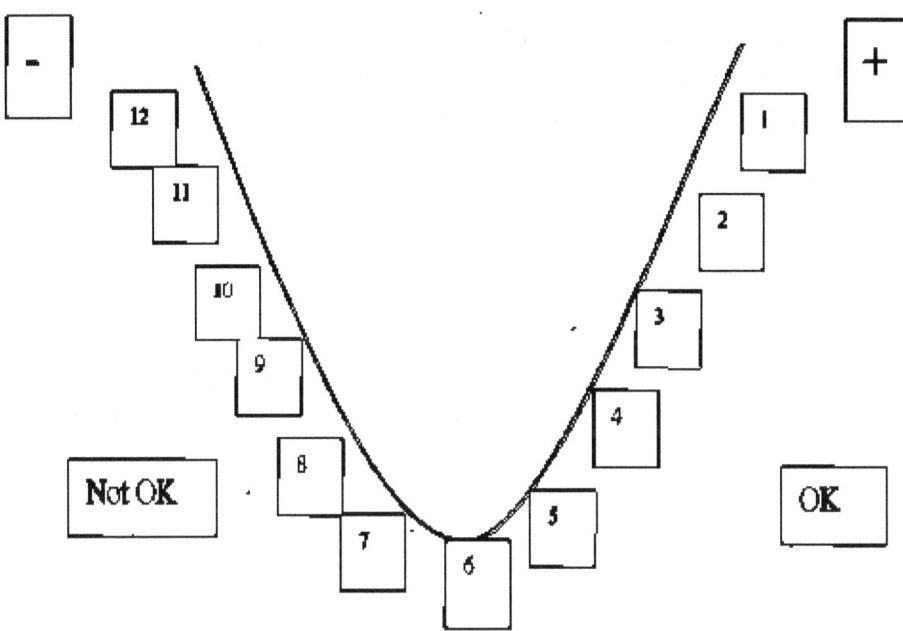

his business? I left him space for his opinions and I went more negative than he did on the pendulum of communication. The only way he could swing was more positive and he did. I could not lose what I did not have and I helped him buy.

Tip:
The Laws of Physics applies to communication, "a body in motion stays in motion", take a risk and keep the pendulum swinging.

CHAPTER 13. UNDERSTAND ALL THE PEOPLE YOU MEET WITH DISC AND MAKE A CONNECTION FASTER.

With the purchase of this book, if you email me at steve@stevelentini.com I will give you a special price for the Everything DiSC for Sales. With DiSC you will learn to first understand your natural character traits and learn how to identify all those you meet and connect with all personality types faster by matching and mirroring the style of communication they prefer.

Bonding is an art and especially for the Spiritual Sales Person. Mindfulness and authenticity are critical. Being fully present, you can make a connection quickly by knowing how to acknowledge your client's space. The way they preferred to be communicated with and DiSC assists you with that.

It is important to learn to mirror body language and tone because together they are 93% of the communication pie. That leaves words with just 7% and understanding who is in front of you, it is easier to match up with them. They feel a connection because you leave your ego at the door and match their style. It is a sign of respect to slow down if you prospect speaks slowly, you slow down. If they speak loud or soft you match it as well because you are present enough to notice it. Some people prefer direct yes or no answers to their questions. Has anyone ever said to you "it was a yes or no question?" Their style is direct... short answers and being present allows you to hear what they prefer.

Some people are very enthusiastic and upbeat and so you match that style. Some are not interested in "getting down to business" quickly... they talk a lot mostly about their job and family and ask you about the same. Engage in the same way and do not get down to business too early, match their pace.

Some people are very skeptical by nature and quiet. When you meet prospect or "future clients" as I like to call them, let them take over. The old rule of client speaks 70% of the time or more does not apply to these people. You ask instead of presenting too early ask "you must have lots of questions about our products or services, so go ahead and ask me?" If you begin by pushing your options you push these people away. They are skeptical of all people they do not know let alone someone who looks a lot like a pushy salesperson.

A spiritual minded sales person understands it is about helping people and letting the skeptical run the sales call. You answer their questions and expect to talk more because you let go of the traditional teaching that says they talk 70% of the time... with skeptics and direct style folks, you can let them drive the call.

If your first thought on every order or presentation is commission, you will see dollars shrink over time and have much slower growth in commission dollars than your counterparts who think "customer's". By staying in the frame of mind that you are there to "help people buy the best solution, even if it's not you", you will grow your sales faster than those salespeople who focus only on their commissions. For your existing customers, do the little things: stay with them on an issue with another department in your company until it is resolved; fix annoying balances that linger on erroneous statements; make that return the customers keeps asking about; care enough to resolve issues that are "someone else's responsibility." Once someone becomes your customer, make them your responsibility, even if the company assigns' another department to do the daily service. Take care of your customer's business and your commissions will grow, especially through referrals from happy customers. Jeffrey Gittomer, author of *The Little Red Book of Selling* says, "If you make a sale, you can earn a commission. If you make a friend, you can earn a fortune".

Thinking "customer first, before commission," will take you to the bank.

TIP: PEOPLE BUY FROM PEOPLE THEY LIKE

and trust. Are you trustworthy?

"Get to know them better if you stand in their shoes"

Steve Lentini

You are first and foremost selling yourself. First impressions are the lasting ones. What is it that you want to portray to the prospects in the first few minutes? People buy from people they like and trust. Your job is to make the prospect comfortable with you. This is where bonding and appearance comes in. Let's start with the bond.

Bonding is one of the keys to sales. In my almost 30 years of coaching, managing, and training sales people, the biggest mistake they made was in the bond. Even though we hear about bonding all the time, many salespeople are unaware that it is how they show up that is their block to selling more. Remember, selling is about them, the prospect, not us.

A. Match and mirror the prospect, stand in their shoes. Begin with body language first. Body language is 55% of the communication pie. Wait for the prospect to begin speaking and match their general posture. Do not play "Simon says" with the prospect. If the prospect is generally relaxed, match it. If they are sitting straight up, match it. This helps you because as you match someone, you get to feel what they are feeling in that same posture and it tells the other person's subconscious that you are like them. Your job is to help people find the right solution and to make them feel at ease with you as soon as possible. Who better to trust than someone who is helping them buy and who is more like them than not?

B. Match their tone and speed of their speech. If they talk soft and slow (usually together), match it. If they talk loudly and fast, pick up your pace and volume. Tonality is 38% of the communication pie.

C. Match their need for bonding. This is most important. If you meet with someone and they want to get right to business and resist your attempts to bond, GET RIGHT TO BUSINESS. Be direct if they are direct. They will like that because it sends a message to their brain, "Hey, this person is just like me." Just follow the prospect's lead, go with the flow. For someone who wants to spend time with you on the bond, allot no more than 20% of the total time set aside for the appointment for the bond. Of a 60-minute call, allow for 12 minutes for bonding.

D. Thoughts have power. They are energy. Scientists' have proven this. Think good thoughts. This sends good energy out from you. You can silently wish your prospect joy, success and happiness. Deepak Chopra, in his book the *Seven Spiritual Laws of Success*, says wishing someone "joy, success and happiness" is akin to bringing someone a gift who has invited you to their home. Hopefully, when invited to someone's home you would bring a gift, but Deepak says that if you did forget, this wish would be just like bringing them an actual gift. Imagine the power of doing this with your prospects.

E. Appearance is critical. Even though the work world has become more relaxed, appearance is critical for successful selling. As far as dress goes, dress professionally. Use common sense and remember the image you want to portray. Matching works here as well. Match the prospect's dress code. When you are setting the appointment ask, "What is the dress code at your office?" What is your dress code saying to the prospect about you and your company? Sloppy dress, sloppy company? Sloppy dress says you have no confidence in your sales ability. The same goes for provocative dress. Dressed professionally, what does that say about you and your company? The same goes with personal hygiene. How do your teeth look? How about your hair? Do you have dandruff? I once coached a guy to wear light sport coats or light plaids to hide his skin condition. He was wearing blue and a dark sport coat and his shoulders and neck looked like a ski resort. You are the first contact with your company that any prospect has. Think about that before you go in.

F. Are you a person of integrity? Do you keep your commitments? Are you on time? Do you return phone calls in a timely fashion? Do you fulfill your promises? Trust is built on integrity. Keep your word everywhere and sell more. It will build trust and help you bond.

G. Forget about that old axiom, "look around the prospect's office to find something to bond about". You can use it if you wish, but prospects are aware of this tactic. Be yourself. I am curious about a person's background so I ask about their background in the company and sometimes I ask if they got recruited in. I will say, "Tell me about your history in this company, did you get recruited in?" That is a subtle pat on the back, a stroke. People are stroke deprived. Most people in top-level management (I hope you are calling on top management) do not get enough strokes. If they were recruited, they usually tell me all about where they came from, and if not, I ask. If where they first started in the company mailroom or at the "bottom," they usually relish in telling me the history as well. It is what I am interested in and that is what I start with. I am naturally curious about people and their careers and how they succeed. Start with an interest of yours; be real and be curious. If you do see a lot of paraphernalia around the office, ask about it, even if you are not a fan; if you are curious, ask. Remember, you do not need a "tacky tactic" if you are being real.

A word of caution though, I once noticed a lot of golf awards in the office of my prospect on a first visit. I said, "Wow, you sure are a great golfer -- three holes in ones?" He replied, "I can't stand golf." I said, "What about all the awards?" He replied, "It's not my office, we know salespeople use this stuff to try and bond so we switch offices here all the time when we have a salesperson come in for a first visit." Beware and ask first, "Is this your office?"

H. Once you ask that question, ("Tell me about your history in this company, did you get recruited in?"), watch what happens. People love to talk about themselves. After a while, with some follow up questions like, "What are your responsibilities?", you can return to selling by asking the prospect, "How can we help you with those responsibilities?"

I. Take notes. Ask permission first. Another stroke. May I take a few notes? Ask this after they have started

SALES SUCCESS FOR THE SPIRITUAL SALESPERSON

sharing what is going on in the company. After you have gathered enough information about their situation, review what they have told you and validate it. It would sound like this. "May I review what you have just told me to be sure I have got it right?" Review and tell them, "This is typically what we are hearing from our customers" (validation by the way). Ask if you missed anything. Ask if they would like to add anything. Then ask, "How do you see an outside company helping you with these issues?" Listen closely, they will tell you how to sell them.

J. Take the pressure off. Tell them that you are there to help them find the right solution, even if it is not you. Ask them if they are okay telling you that you are not the right fit for them. Tell them that you are okay with *no*. This is taking the pressure off both of you. It is reminding you that that is why you are there, to see if

it is a fit for both of you. Then you could say, "If I sense that your company is not a fit for us, would you mind if I say that?" After all, we do not sell everyone.

Tip:
Be fully present and
mindful - bonding will come
naturally to you

CHAPTER 14 : DETACH FROM OUTCOMES

> ***Tip:**
> Selling becomes easier when you go with the flow.

D

Detaching from outcomes helps you relax in the middle of the action. How can you lose what you do not have? Being detached from
outcomes, you can help people buy and be comfortable. Being detached will help you take risks with evasive buyers. How can you take a huge risk if you are attached and worried about not getting the sale?

> **Tip:**
> You cannot lose what you do not have.

Remember, you do not have it. Take a risk. I spent many years attempting to control other people and thankfully realized what a waste of energy it was.

> *"After you learn to detach, relax and go with the flow, life works better everywhere"*
>
> *Steve Lentini*

Being detached from outcomes helps you with rejection. How can you be rejected if you are not attached to the outcome? View everything as just an event, not good or bad, just outcomes. Since you cannot control outcomes in life, only yourself, focus on what you can control. YOU!

When you sense things are not going where you wanted, do not push too hard, unless you are in front of a hard driving person. Let the customer know you can see that you've missed something, then ask directly: "What did I miss? How can we get back on track?" Watch for the telltale signs that you have upset someone. Notice body language. Is the prospect closing up? Is he/she moving away from you, pursing lips, furrowing their brow, or worse, crossing their arms and moving away from you at the same time? If there is anything that you sense, even a feeling that you have said something that upset them, find a way to say what you feel or see. Be prepared to soften the question first. People love to help people, so struggle on purpose if you must. If you are feeling uncomfortable, share that. You could say, "I am feeling like you are upset, I could be wrong, tell me, are you uncomfortable with this purchase, or with me?" Give them a chance to respond. Whatever it is! It could even be, "Well, I get the sense that we are not a fit. Are you feeling the same way?"

Your goal is to help people buy. Some prospects buy because of force or they are tired of pestering. They do anything to get away from the constant barrage of phone calls and

emails. These prospects do not stay customers for long. Often, they change their mind within 24 hours and cancel orders. Have you had, what you thought was an enthusiastic prospect, say that "things really looked good" and even after saying: "Call me on Monday and I'll give you an order," they still did not return your calls? It could be because you put too much pressure on them and you did not realize it. If this was the case, the prospect just wanted to be rid of you. They do not return calls. Do your research on this. Customers, given respect and the space to buy what fits, will stay your customers.

You waste energy pushing a customer who is a soft personality type when they have decided it's a "no sale". It's your fault you missed something - use the energy instead to discover what you have missed or to move on to a new customer. Do the both of you a favor and voluntarily close a presentation that is going nowhere. Many times recognizing the ending opens real dialogue that might get a sale. So, go with the flow. You are easier to be around and you will attract new outcomes.

The only exception to the above is when you are dealing with hard driving personality types. You must match and mirror them -- push them, prod them, give them back what they give you just as hard or harder -- they will like and respect you for it.

CHAPTER 15: DO NOT SETTLE FOR LESS

Don't cave in to the Income Avalanche. Spiritual salespeople have faith in something bigger in the Universe, whatever they call it. With faith there is no fear that you will not have enough in the world. With fear that you will not have enough income, you make poor decisions on business prospects, accepting customers who drain energy. Doing business with inappropriate types of people does not work. While you are running around meeting the demands of these customers, who you have trained to take advantage of you, you could be working with people who will allow you to make an abundant living. If you have not helped customers grow, then do so now. Make them more profitable. Maybe you could gradually raise their prices.

> **Tip: You are always harvesting something you planted. If you want a bigger harvest, Plant more!**

Educate customers on what makes your company more productive and hence able to offer the most competitive programs.

I remade my whole territory one year by asking myself: "who

would you call on, who would you sell if you did not worry about money?"

If you would do something different, then you could make the change. If you said, like I did, "I have the greatest job in the world, and I'd change this or that" - then write down the changes. See how you can live up to them, then give yourself a timetable to make the changes happen.

I used this plan to remake my own territory and followed with two record-setting years and the "Salesperson of the Year" award.

Starting with the end in mind, I thought about what needed improving in my territory. I wanted to deal with larger customers and make 100% more than I was making and have more time to myself to enjoy life. Next, I reviewed each customer and ranked them by sales, profit, commission and the time they required from me. I noticed that many of the low margin customers took a lot of my time. I also noticed that some of the large customers required that I showed up each week. I knew that to get more time to see new, larger customers or to increase sales in my best customers, I would have to re-arrange the time I was spending and increase the margins on many of my existing customers.

Next, I targeted those customers that had the potential to grow and those that needed a reduced call schedule and higher margins.

I set meetings with each client and told them upfront that my company wants to increase sales by 20% or more during the next 12 months. I then told them of my new plans. If it involved calling on them in person only once per month, instead of weekly, we discussed it. I asked how they felt, and together we settled on how we would make it work. I set phone calls in between, or trained some of their staff to place the orders, etc.

Price is not why people buy.

**Tip:
Customers will say price is key.

Setting the expectation upfront will

determine if you get your price or not.**

1. Begin upfront with prospects and set the pricing expectation. I would always say, "We are not the lowest price. We focus on good service and results. Would you agree that we usually get what we pay for in life?" or "How do you price your products? Are you the lowest price provider in your business?" Usually their answer here was *no*, and I would add, "Well, neither are we". If they did answer *yes* then perhaps they would not be a fit for me and I would ask more questions to determine a fit like "Is price the only factor you use when deciding on a purchase like this?", etc.

2. Starting with the end in mind, what is the ideal margin you require to provide your customer with the level of service they expect and that aligns with your

mission statement? Do the research. Where are your company's products or services priced in relation to your competition? If you are the lowest or close, why not go up 5%? Raise prices by 10% on all services and items that your customers buy because you have it or that you sell very few of each month. They are buying because you have it or you are particularly good at it. What is your market' share? If it's below 2% or above 30% you could raise pricing. If you are on the lower share of the market, you can raise prices because lowering 5% will not raise your market' share significantly and could put you out of business. Hopefully, your service or your mission justifies the increase. If you are on the higher end of market' share, determine why you have achieved that proportion of share? Perhaps you have the reputation for great service and can justify a 2 – 5% higher margin. Test it -- have your marketing staff do the survey or hire someone to do it. If they justify the increase, you can get a quick return on that investment.

Get your price. Here is how:

Pay full price when you shop. Be willing to pay top dollar to a merchant you like. Pay for a service from a merchant who earns your trust and respect. What we give we get in life, so if you want full price, be willing to pay it. I have worked with sales people who complain about customers or prospects being focused only on price and when I inquire about how they buy something or ask them to tell me about the last time they bought a car, they often have quite a story about how they really "worked the sales person" and got a really good deal. Are you always bragging about how you got a low price?

SET THE INTENTION FOR WHAT YOU WANT;

Albert Einstein said "Intention is responsible for 80% of the creation of matter"

He also said "Everything is determined...by forces over which we have no control."

Use affirmations to reinforce your intention. A good affirmation is "I am trusted, I give great service and I am paid full price." Get Wayne Dyers' book, *The Power of Intention*. Use your imagination. Visualize contracts signed and handshakes with those margins agreed upon. See the happy faces of your prospects. Feel what it would feel like to have outcomes like these. Use the power of your thoughts to help you create the world you envision.

Tip:
Use your imagination, see yourself

3.   Be prepared to say no if the price the prospect is attempting to negotiate is below your margin bottom line, below what you determined what you could say yes to. Say, "we wouldn't be able to say yes to that... (pause) it would mean we would have to cut our service somewhere. I could cut somewhere in the proposal. What would be okay to cut back on?" Walk away from it if you must. Prospects respect your boundaries and if they do not, you do not need them. Many times I have held my line on pricing and walked, only to have the prospect either hold me from leaving or call me up a day or so later to say, "I have a purchase order for you, would you come in to discuss the final details?" Real negotiations begin at *no.*

5. Read the book *Blue Ocean Strategy.* Create a Blue Ocean Strategy for your company and get your margins without hesitation because you are serving a market that has customers calling you for your expertise. You are not another "me too", selling the same product or service where price becomes the major determining factor.

6. If you decide to operate in the low-price arena, get your operation lean, mean, efficient and productive; give great service, low pricing, and make a profit at the same time.

Your market, your territory is what you have made it

You can remake your company or your territory anytime you like.

Here is how:

1. Start with the end in mind, as Stephen Covey says, "Set your annual income goal."

2. What is the average sale for the territory? How many customers or sales are required to hit the goal? What if the average sale doubled? What kind of prospects or customers fit the profile of doubling the average sale? How many of the existing customers fit the profile of the increased average sale? Make a list of the existing customers that do not fit your new profile. Determine which customers have the potential to fit your new profile over time. Perhaps they are buying from some of your competitors and you could increase your business or they are growing or have plans for expansion. Any customers that will not fit your new plan, give them to someone else in the company, perhaps a trainee or decide to make phone calls the main source of contact with your customers . You could raise their prices and just see what happens.

Next, using the picture of your new, ideal customer, make a list of target accounts. Ask your existing customers if they know anyone who works at these accounts and would they recommend you?

Would they introduce you to them?

Even if the person they know is not the decision maker, their friend or contact would probably know the decision maker or know someone at the company who does. Either way, you get to make a warm call, instead of a cold call. Next, for targets that you cannot get introduced into, develop a marketing post card, something that would get their attention concerning your product or service. Perhaps you know of a problem or pain that many of your customers had before you sold them. Send the post card or email to the target accounts

(email or mail 20 or 25 at a time, it's easier to follow up on a small amount, remember to keep it manageable)

Email or mail them three or four times and be sure to include the following message on the third and fourth attempt, "I will be calling you to ask for an appointment next week."

Now, make sure that you call. Your goal is to keep the emailing and mailing going with new targets so that eventually you will be calling 20 to 25 targets per week, 4 or 5 per day -- manageable. Your job is action. Keep the action up and sales will increase.

3. Cold calls. If you are going to cold call, make them outrageous. The targets should be the best of the best. Start at the top. Call the president. Who calls her or him anyway? Very few people start at the top. Call on prospects that you have previously thought would never buy from you. Even the ones that you think the competition has "sewn up". If you only make one of these calls per day, that equals five per week. Over the course of 50 weeks, that is 250

calls per year. If you only get 20 appointments and close 5, you are closing 5 of your targets from the list of the "best of the best" customers that buy what you sell. Imagine the impact of that one activity on your sales results. Imagine the impact on your income. Feel how it would feel. How would your company feel about you? Feel it. It is behavior that gets results over time. Keep working and forget about outcomes. If you are working each day and working on yourself as well, the outcomes will be positive.

CHAPTER 15: DEVELOP A SYSTEM TO FOLLOW

Prospects have been using a system designed as a defensive measure against high pressure and nonprofessional salespeople.

Does this sound familiar? Prospects tell you that they are very interested and ask you to tell them all about your company and what you sell. You tell them and ask for the order. They start to work you on price or ask you to do a quote or formal proposal. You do one and again ask for the order. They tell you it looks good and ask you to call back in a week or so. You do and you get stuck in what I call voice mail jail.

Prospects are either using you to get a better price from their current supplier or service provider; or they are getting free consulting.

I suggest that you use a system to help you determine if prospects are really committed to what you provide. Then you could decide to move forward or not; and you will be helping them make the same decision as well. Help them buy. You could use my suggested system that follows or develop one of your own. Remember that your prospects are using one, so be prepared.

1. Bond

Set aside 20% of the allotted time for the call to bond, unless the client shows no inclination to bond.

2. Set the rules of the call. Set an agenda.

Have an outline or agenda. Tell them "to help make our time together productive, I have an agenda, would you mind if I go over it?" Tell them that you will have to ask what might seem like a lot of questions, to help them determine if you are the right company for them. Give them permission to ask you questions as well. Tell them that in your experience, most people ask a lot of questions as well and some of them are… (Suggest some questions, ones that you would like them to ask!).

3. Provide pressure relief.

Then say, "If at any point you feel like my company is not a good fit, do you mind telling me 'no, it's not going to work'? I'm okay with *no*." After they respond, you could also add, "On the other hand, we do not do business with everyone. Would you mind if I came to the same conclusion if I said, 'Gee, I get a feeling that you are not a fit for us, do you mind if I share why?'" (This could pave the way to reopen the sale).

4. Use the 70/30 rule. This is time for your questions.

Use the 70/30 gauge commitment. What you are feeling, find a way to say it. Bring up your biggest fears.

Prepare questions that will encourage the prospect to talk 70% of the time. Listen and take notes to gauge for areas of pain or concern. Listen for problems that are potentially costing them lots of money if they do not fix them. Listen for problems that could cost them their job, company, or prestige if they ignore them. Listen for a desire to have a new future, unlike the past. Ask about the past, how long have they had the problem? What have they done to fix it? Has it worked? Have they told their existing supplier? What happened?

If the responses have them telling you a story of woe, ask them how they feel about that. Whatever you feel during their responses, find a way to say it and whatever your biggest fears are, bring them up.

This builds an adult-adult relationship. People will respect you for it. Refer to the communication chart in Key 9. [What is Key 9? Maybe list the page number instead.]

5. Determine budget.

> **Tip:**
> X should be higher than your lowest price.

Ask, in general terms, what have they set aside to fix the problem?

If they respond with "We never share that." ask "If I said it was going to cost between X and Y, are you in that range? Closer to X?

6. Decision, ask about the decision process.

Ask "The last time you made a decision like this, what did that process look like? Will you be bringing anyone else in to help you?" (If yes, ask if they are there now, or when will they be including them in a meeting.) Suggest that typically, you attend the final decision meeting to help them all make the best decision for their business. Ask how do they see you helping them make the decision?

7. Time to present

Present only to the needs expressed during the questioning, nothing more, and nothing less. Before you start, ask if you can go over your notes to be sure you have all of their concerns correct. Go over the list and validate their concerns, "We see this..." Ask if they have anything to add, then ask them to rank their top three of the ones you went over.

You only need the top three to start your presentation. Start with the top three.

8. Close.

Take the temperature first. Ask "on a scale of 0 to 10, if 0 was we would not go to the next step, and 8 was we would go to the next step, where are you on that scale?" If over 5, ask, "what would you need to hear to go to 8?" If they are below 5 ask "what would you need to hear to get to a 5? If they are at 8, simply ask, "What would you like to do next?" They will tell you how to close them.

If they are at 0, you could say, "Oh, I must have missed something, where did you feel that we were not a fit?" Listen intently as you could reopen or it could be the time to end it as well. If you have great questions and develop a great back and forth dialogue with the customer, you could close by asking "I'm curious, what do you think is the next step for you?" In fact, I have had clients ask me that after a back and forth communication that included the upfront, pressure relief, and they knew that I had their best interest in mind. They closed the sale because they also sensed my authentic energy and my integrity, that I would do what was best for them.

9. Set the deal.

Be sure the deal is set. Once you close, hand the purchase order or deposit check back to the prospect before you go, and ask, "Sometimes, not very often, people change their minds for various reasons after I leave, is there anything else you think we need to cover before I take your (check or Po)?" This gives the prospect the chance to deal with buyer's remorse before you go. Did you ever leave a store thinking, "Why did I buy that?" Discover if your prospects are feeling any remorse over their decision and help them with it. If you are detached from outcomes, you can bring this up easily and prospects will thank you for it.

Remember during the whole interview, whatever you feel, whatever you fear, pay attention to it. Find a way to say it.

10. Keep track of your results.

Track how you are doing and use a system. Whether you choose this one or another, using a system can help you figure out what you may be doing wrong, but only if you track your results and when you lose an opportunity you diagnose what went wrong by going back over your notes and reviewing what step you missed something or perhaps rushed through it. You could always ask the client later, after a few weeks, what happened. Get their feedback about what you missed or what you could have done better.

> **Tip:**
> You cannot manage what you do not measure.

CHAPTER 16: SOCIAL MEDIA – GET IT RIGHT.

I like LinkedIn and Twitter, and the rules apply for any of the social media you choose for business. What follows is my advice.

What not to do after you connect with someone.

The following is based on my experience. The events described below are real. The names have been removed to protect the innocent

1. Don't reach out to me like this after just connecting with me;

"Good evening, I just read your profile and l thought this is something you might be interested in. A reputable partner of mine is proposing to collaborate with you in a profitable business arrangement that is very much within your capacity as an individual or business owner to accomplish.

For more information, contact xxxxxxxxxxxxxxxxxx

Awaiting your response and please all inquiry should be sent via e-mail to xxxxxxxxx as I will be away for a family vacation. Do have a great weekend ahead.

Warm Regards".

Can you believe it? Would you accept this request? How did you feel about it while you read it? I do not know the person. The lack of professionalism and can you smell the commission breath?

Amazing, huh? Respect your connections and get to know them first.

2. You have just connected or I have agreed to connect with you, and we do not know each other. Why would you recommend me? I am not flattered easily, and less so by people who have never met me and they recommend me for my skills -- or management ability or sales ability. Perhaps you could recommend me for writing skills after you read some of my work, but how could you for anything else? Again, get to know me first.

3. Please don't reach out with an offer to sell me a product or service. Again, I don't know you and people buy from people they like and trust. Build trust first with an offer to help me or send me some information you think will help me. Do not sell me too early as I just dismiss all of those requests. Did you even read that I am a sales trainer and author? At least do some research and find out my philosophy of selling -- I am all over the web.

4. Download *The 7 Habits of Highly Successful LinkedIn Users* by Dennis Brown or *LinkedIn the Sandler Way* by Sandler Sales Training at https://www.sandler.com/resources/sandler-books/LinkedIn-social-selling

   Study how to use LinkedIn from a few experts before you do any prospecting.

   I am glad to help you after you connect with me. Ask me for help; it's another way for us to get to know each other.

Then maybe we would recommend each other or refer each other.

I want to get to know you. Reach out like that and I am glad to help.

LinkedIn, Twitter or any Social Media are perfect for helping people buy. You can write articles about what you sell and how to get the best value. You can tweet articles that are related to your industry. You become visible through writing and then become credible by your content. Dr. Ivan Mizner, Founder of BNI says, "Visibility + Credibility = Profitability."

As I have said, "no commission breath" -- no one cares about your need to make a quota or a raise in pay. Remember, the energy you put out comes back. What did you think about the people I wrote about above? How would you describe the energy they put out?

Relax, breathe, and add value. It will come back. You will be a respected expert in your industry over time. Malcom Gladwell wrote, "This is the scholarly tradition I was referring to in my book *Outliers*, when I wrote about the 'ten-thousand-hour rule.' No one succeeds at a high level without innate talent, I wrote: 'achievement is talent plus preparation.'" But the ten-thousand-hour research reminds us that "the closer psychologists look at the careers of the gifted, the smaller the role innate talent seems to play and the bigger the role preparation seems to play." He goes on to say, "Anyone could achieve a level of proficiency that would rival that of a professional. It was just a matter of putting in the time."

Put in the time to become an expert and people will come to you. If you push your product or your expertise, there is only one way people can go, and that is away from pushing.

When you use the great gift of productivity, along with properly using Social Media to help people buy, that energy will draw people to you.

A spiritual salesperson has integrity and they know helping others is a good energy that resonates throughout the world and the universe without expecting return in kind. Just knowing that it does come back because of the Law "You get what you give". Help others and watch what happens. Do not take my word for it... experiment by putting out the energy of helping and giving for a few years and see what happens. Prove this to yourself.

CHAPTER 10: MLM; MULTI-LEVEL MARKETING SALES

I have been in a few multi-level marketing sales businesses. I have been solicited by many others who wanted me to participate as a "business owner" or as a customer. Many used pressure tactics "pushing me" (or thinking they were) to enroll me in their program. Telling anyone how great your program is -- how great your shake is or promising what your skin cream can do -- makes me want to puke and run away. When you sell too hard, it's now all about your goals. How do you think I feel when you are pushing to sell "your products?"

I know a few MLM folks who push, push, push. I have heard them say, "I don't get it Steve...this is a no brainer, why don't they see that and want to join in or buy the product...I just don't get it."

The only thing that these folks don't get is the history of MLM. There have been many flops along with all of the successes. Typically, MLM people approach non sales people who are uncomfortable with any kind of approaching people about anything -- it's not personal. When any kind of pressure is put on the nonsleepers, they will say anything to get you away from them, including things like "Okay this sounds great, I will be doing it...call me next Tuesday and I will sign up." Or "Yes it sounds great, let me think about it and call me tomorrow." Sound familiar?

I know they do. These kind of responses come from a lack of upfront
work, softening your approach and wanting your goals more than you want to help your friend, your relative or your prospect.

If you love your MLM program, whether it's energy, shakes, vitamins or whatever, you want folks to experience what you love -- and you want them to feel that. Make sure whatever you choose is in total alignment with your higher sense, your spiritual self.

Here is how to help people experience your passion, and not your goals.

1. Make sure that this MLM is truly your passion. Make sure that you have a story, a true story, about how this work or product has changed your life. What your life was before and now after.

Detach from outcomes. I have talked about that in previous chapters and it is the same with MLM. You cannot control others, only yourself; so discernment and discipline is especially important now with MLM. Ask questions that bring up your biggest fears like "What have you heard about MLM's in general, how do you feel about MLM, and what experience have you had previously with people who were in a MLM and approached you? What about approaching others, how do you feel? Would you like to hear about how this has changed my life and how I feel when I help others with this? Would you like to hear about how others who I have successfully helped? How about those that did not make it?" (all MLM folks have people who have enrolled and did not do much or anything at all after enrolling). Get the point? You are curious about where your friend, relative or prospect stands and how they feel, not starting with how great your program is. It's about establishing a dialogue that helps them hear and you, if they are even a fit...help them hear their own fears and then you help them... Hopefully your program has an effective program for building a relationship not a sale. Sales will come if you follow my program or any good program. It's easy...be human, be vulnerable and be there to help.

2. Now you ask, "Would you like to hear how I help my fellow partners?" Now talk about what you do to help your fellow MLM partners succeed. Do you have such a program or are you only interested in signing folks up? Here is where the rubber meets the road -- if you are not interested in helping your downline succeed, then this is truly about your goals and your greed. Rethink this, as it will be a huge stumbling block down the road. Create a program to help others succeed and remember, you get what you give. Success will come to you

3. "Would you like me to show you our program?" Now you show your program, all along the way asking permission to move ahead. Check by taking it away, and not as a tactic, but because you care, you ask, "How are you feeling about this so far? Would you like to say *no* now? Am I scaring you at all? Okay to move ahead?" Now you share your program in all its glory.

4. After your presentation, ask "Okay, who wants to leave?" Never be afraid of *no*. *No* helps you get those who can be a fit and a *yes* faster to *yes*. *No's* will be a *no* anyway. When would you like to know it? If anyone says "Yes, I want to leave..." you say, "Okay, would you mind sharing why and what makes you uncomfortable?" Once they answer, you could ask, "What would make you feel more comfortable?

If you can reopen it, fine. Otherwise, let them go. I would ask, "Anyone else feel the same way?" When you are not afraid to have anyone in the room who does not want to be there, guess who remains? Those who are really interested and they see how that is your goal. Your true goal is to help others succeed and not to "force" anyone to sign up. Either they get it or it's okay not to.

5. Now you say to those remaining... "Okay, any other questions?" and then "Okay, those who would like to know what is next, come on up."

6. For those who do sign up, you ask, "Okay, before I complete the enrollment, are you sure, how do you feel right now? Again, you cannot lose someone who is really committed and feels the same passion and has a dream or a goal to be in the same MLM business as you. You will be amazed at how this process works, and then ask people "How was my process for you? Do you feel like you can learn it? I want you to learn how to help others decide to do this, not to sell anyone on doing this. Okay?"

If you would like me to speak to your group about this method of connecting with people, call me or email me. steve@stevelentini.com or call me at 917-805-1088.

CHAPTER 17: SEEDS OF SUCCESS

"We are always harvesting something we planted"

- Steve Lentini

Use the examples that Nature provides all around us for free.

Nature provides us with a powerful example of how to have an abundant harvest. In nature, we see four distinct seasons. Spring, Summer, Fall and Winter.

In Spring, the farmer prepares the ground for the planting of the seeds. The salesperson in spring is preparing the ground for his/her future success. How does a salesperson prepare the ground? Make meeting new people every day your goal, not selling them. Your purpose in spring is to prepare the ground and to plant the seeds. Resist the urge to "rush the harvest". Too often, salespeople attempt selling, or harvesting, the first time they call or meet someone. Prospects usually "pull back" from early attempts to "harvest" or sell. They feel the pressure. Would you stand over a tomato seedling and shout, "Okay now, give me a tomato!"? Of course not. We understand the cycles in nature much better than we do with people, and yet the laws are the same. Prepare the ground, plant the seed and then wait. The same goes for selling. Prepare the ground with research about where your ideal customers hang out. Then plant seeds by meeting them there, where they hang out. You can also prepare the ground with effective marketing, mailing and advertising campaigns. Good public relations and community work also helps, especially when your efforts get noticed and published in the newspapers or in the media.

CARE FOR YOUR CUSTOMERS; GIVE THEM THE SERVICE THEY DESERVE; WEED AND FEED

Do the research and prepare the ground. Then plant seeds by meeting people and making relationships first.

Find out how you can help people. Discipline your thoughts and judgments when you first meet people. Think only good thoughts. I silently salute the "Divinity" in each person I meet every day, and I send them my blessings as a gift or I wish them "joy, success and happiness". Thoughts have energy, so sending positive thoughts to your prospects, clients, friends and relatives couldn't hurt. Think of the times that you have called someone and noticed that they did not seem okay. How did you notice? You felt that their energy was lowered or heard something in their voice that said things weren't right. Customers and prospects will pick up on the energy that you are sending when you are thinking positive thoughts about them.

After the seeds sprout in spring, next comes the summer.

Think care, nurture, feed and weed
Summer is a time for care of the crop. The seeds of spring have broken through the hard ground. Now is the time for consistent effort. Care for your customers. Little time off and much diligence is required. Protection of the crops, nurturing, feeding, and weeding are the daily routines to provide for the growth into strong plants, or customers, that will give the bountiful harvest. Again, you will face many tests as nature deems you fit, or not, for the upcoming harvest. "Will you rail against the storms, rocks, bugs and weeds?" as Jim Rohn says in his book *The Garden of Life*. Call them unfair and unjust? If so, you are classified as one who seeks the reward without the effort, something in return for nothing. In our Cause and Effect Universe, this cannot be. If you expect something for nothing, you will reap just that. It is not unfair; it is just how it is. The Universe does not weep for your failure or celebrate your victory. If

after planting your seeds, you do not see results, the lesson here is to persist through the doubt. Keep your vision. Take some time daily to visualize your goals. Imagine contracts being signed and checks coming to you. I spend time daily actually "seeing" the checks, using my imagination. I imagine the check. In my

mind's eye I see "Pay to the order of." I see the amounts made out, then the written amount and the check signed. I see "handshake deals and contracts signed".

*Tip: "Diamonds are made with a combination of extreme pressure and abrasion."

Expect to be tested. As humans grow strong by facing obstacles and difficulty. Resistance in life grows our muscles for living. Gratitude and action is required for all of our adversity. For our character grows with adversity and in our response to it, not with inaction. As we come to expect difficulty, we can celebrate our future strength and see that in the absence of adversity, we would wither and be blown away with the first "storms of our lives".

I heard a story about the "Biosphere" in Colorado. When it first opened, under a dome, it was a grand experiment. Scientists were duplicating everything in nature under a dome to observe all the cycles of life for possible life on far away planets. The idea was that, if it worked, we could duplicate our life on barren planets, under a controlled environment like the dome. Scientists noticed the trees that were planted, would fall over when they reached between five and six feet tall. They were scrawny and not very healthy looking. They tried different foods, tested the soils, varied the temperatures and the light conditions, but nothing worked. Then, one day someone realized what had been missing. Wind! Varied winds, especially strong winds, served to break some of the roots as the trees s wayed back and forth in response.

Where the roots broke, new shoots formed which went deeper into the ground, serving to further anchor the tree to protect it from future high winds and storms. So to, storms and the high winds of our lives allow us to form more deeper roots. With this new appreciation for our storms, we can be grateful when they come. We can know deep down that we are being prepared and strengthened for a future bountiful harvest. What a gift.

There is a long anticipated return for what we have sown. What we (competitors) who would take and watch out for pests have now in our lives is our harvest your harvest. Pay attention. from our previous s pring. Whatever our preparation was, whatever seeds we planted, we are now reaping. If you are frustrated, unhappy, broke, unemployed or deeply in debt, you have planted the seeds of this yourself. Accept the responsibility and move on.

You could blame others for your harvest, but if you planted a garden and it withered and died, or if you neglected it and the harvest was meager, would you blame it on your employer, your parents, your spouse, your business partners, or any others? Of course not, and yet we see humans attempt to do this with their lives all the time. Until we let go of the "blame game", the victim, and the pity mode, we cannot advance to a rich and bountiful harvest. The harvest is a time to let go of things.

Just as the trees let go of the leaves,   just as the blossoms and fruits fall we too must decide what who to let go of in our lives. To have a new future you must decide to let go of old patterns and choices that have held us to this harvest of gloom. And yet this is also a reason to celebrate. Because whatever our current harvests, we can begin to plant anew.

> "If you don't like your experience of the world, change how the world is experiencing you" Steve Lentini

Winter, don't forget to rest

Winter is our time to rest, to surrender. Surrender to the idea that things are still happening underground, although we cannot see them. Before planting anew, after any harvest, a time of reflection is required. Winter is a time of learning too. A time for seminars, classes and study of what could be next. Meditation about what did not work in the last harvest, what did, and preparation and planning for the next planting is important too. Winter is a good time for journaling. Write down what the recent harvest brought in to the storehouse or the lack of it. Tie the resultant harvest back to the activities and action we took in spring. Notice any patterns of self-doubt and defeat. Look for the "blame game" and victim dialogue within yourself. Even if you have just had a bountiful harvest, one cannot assume that this pattern will repeat. You must take the same care with planting the next crop, selecting the site, soil, and seeds carefully, so as to ensure another bountiful harvest.

We humans are built to grow, expand and produce. We are happiest when we are risking and reaching deep down within ourselves, using all of our gifts. Magnanimity is joyful. Pusillanimity is not. Pusillanimity is holding back one's gifts. The Universe knows that you are holding out. Dare and dream big. Believe. Now is the time to prepare for when the earth warms and the soil loosens. Getting ready for the slip and slide from the mud of spring, the high winds and the rains.

Preparation now will make winters enjoyable as you will see the need for winter in your cycle. You will understand winter's role and be grateful for it. Unlike our western society, where rest is scorned, you will come to value it as you rest and prepare for the next planting, while others are still running around wondering what just happened in the last harvest -- not even aware that the cycles and seasons of nature are here to teach, instruct and even comfort us. We can be comforted knowing that cycles and seasons are normal and a part of our lives as well, not just something to go through or complain about each year.*

*information on the seasons comes from Toni Stone, c/o Wonder Works Studio, 401 Buck Hollow Road, Fairfax, Vt, wwwwonderworks.org and from Jim Rohn's book *The Seasons of Life*

CHAPTER 18: NETWORKING

I once worked for a company that needed quick sales growth and the President's father had a contact in a large potential customer that we wanted badly. I'll never forget that call in my life.

On the day of the appointment, we spent three minutes or less on small talk, even though Arthur could have spent an hour catching up with his old friend. I almost fell off of my chair when Arthur asked, "Would you give my friend, Steve, some business?" - Now his friend had two options, either *yes* or *no*. He said, "yes"!

It might have taken me six months to get to that point with this very large company, but Arthur knew he could be direct with his very good business friend. I use this story often when I'm in front of a group of salespeople because it illustrates the value of using contacts and referrals. Going over your contact list every three to six months and asking your customers, friends, and acquaintances for referrals should be on going. Use any "tool" in your toolbox to shorten that decision cycle. Offer your help on a regular basis to your contacts. Watch out for business opportunities for your clients. Give them referrals often. You get what you give.

Help others with your contacts, Ralph Waldo Emerson, in his "Essay on Compensation" said, "The undisputable law of this Universe is that you get what you give."(There's that law again). If you want people to give you referrals, give them. Your book antennae should always be up for opportunities to help others. Help your customers and prospects that you meet do more business; be ready to introduce others to them that will help them. Help other sales people that you know grow their business and they will want to help you.

Networking fits in with this strategy because it's giving to others. In networking, you shall reap as you sow. Cold calling is a waste of time, in my opinion. The return for the time spent is often very low when you add in the burn out factor. Sales people, who rely solely on cold calling, burn out and turnover at a very high rate. We know this and yet most sales training is still focused on cold calling. If you are going to cold call, make it five a day on outrageously big targets.

Set your sights on the biggest and best customers you can dream of and cold call them. Call the President. That way, the risk and reward ratio makes the effort worthwhile.

The same could apply to your networking. You could be working with the best and brightest in similar industries, helping them to get business. Sowing this, you would reap, over time, a harvest of the best and brightest people helping you and introducing you to new prospects. The difference is that with networking, you would be invited in, and perhaps even personally introduced, at a lunch or dinner meeting. Even one warm call a week would beat the best week of cold calling. The key to effective networking is effective sowing. I hear people complain "I'm not getting anything from my group." What do you think they sowed in spring to reap a harvest of "not getting anything"? The rule does not apply sometimes; it applies every time. As Dr. Ivan Misner, founder of BNI (Business Networking International) says, "Givers Gain. That is the motto of BNI."

Start by selecting your sites to plant. Would you plant a garden in a field of rocks, thorns, trees and scrub bushes?

Do some research;

Ask questions. Look for groups that fit your particular occupation or business. Once selected, attend a few meetings to be sure that they call on similar types of customers and do not compete with you. How do they present themselves? How do they dress? Do they behave professionally? Would you refer these people? What are they sowing in the world? If they are sloppy and careless with their dress and their words, what kind of clients and prospects do you think are part of their harvest? Take your time here and do the due diligence. When you have found the group that fits, plant the seed and join. Now begins the springtime of your membership. Things will look messy here. The beginning of your membership in any group will feel that way. Take time here to plant deeply and carefully. Meet each member out for breakfast or lunch. Find out how you can help them. Be prepared for the meeting. Show them how professional you are. Keep your word and do everything you say you will do, even if it hurts. Do not break appointments, arrive late, or worse, arrive unprepared. Take notes in your meeting. Note the personal facts like birthdays, anniversaries, children's names, spouse name, and quirky facts that you can acknowledge at a later date. Remember, you are sowing here. Also, be aware during the meeting if the person is interested in what you do. Are they asking how they could help you? Remember, they will be showing you how they sow a crop as well. If they do not reflect the kind of crop that you want to plant, offer to help them with some ideas that you have about growing their business or better, give them this book. If they still do not fit, tell them why, and if they are open to help, give it. If not, move on to preserve your future harvest. If you feel good about working with the person, work on getting them a referral or introduction. Offer to link their website to yours. Feature them or their business in your newsletter. Send a personal letter introducing them to your top 10 customers. As you work to help them plant, so will you reap the same. Be patient. No rushing to the harvest.

Instead of joining a group to network in, you could do the same with a few respected business people who you know or would like to know, that call on the same types of customers as you and you do not compete with them. You could call them and say that you respect them, have heard great things about them, and that you call on similar types of customers.

Note that you do not compete and that you were thinking that you could help them grow their business. Suggest that you meet for lunch. Start the same process as above. The goal would be to find four or five people that you could work with to develop what BNI calls a contact sphere.

The key to prospecting is setting a goal of "warming up" the calls. Offer seminars that educate your prospect; do not sell at these events. Warm calls require that you get to know your

prospect, and they get to know you. Whatever your industry, offer an informative seminar educating on an important aspect of what you do. Give real information. What you give, you get. When you give real information, your prospects will learn something and appreciate that you did not attempt to sell them. At the beginning of the seminar, ask the attendees to take out a business card and turn it over. Ask them to put the letters Y N TIO on the card. At the end of the seminar tell them what the letters stand for. Y = yes, N = no, TIO = think it over. Tell them to cross out think it over unless they are willing to accept a call from you within 48 hours and tell you *yes* or *no*. Under those circumstances, it would be okay to circle TIO. If not, then they must circle *Yes* or *No*. Tell the *no*'s you will call to ask what they liked about the seminar and to ask what could have been improved. Tell them that they can circle *yes* if they would like to hear more about what you taught them. Tell them that you will call to set an appointment.

Design a post card or an ad that you can mail or email to target prospects. Most people at least look at a postcard to decide whether to throw it out or delete it. Email it or mail it to the top 15 or 20 prospects on your list each week for four weeks and then call. You can ask if they have gotten your postcard. You can ask if they remember throwing out the one that looked like yours. Again the goal is to warm up the call.

Go over your customer list and ask for referrals. Do this every six months or so. Ask your top customers how you can help them get business. What is it that they are looking for? You cannot do this for everyone, although your top customers would appreciate a referral too. And remember, you get what you give.

Think of ways to warm up the call first, then call. By making your daily goal of meeting say five new people that you can discover whether or not they

> **Tip:**
> Make your daily goal to meet new people and HAVE FUN.

ever buy what you sell, you take the pressure off of yourself to sell something right away.

You are new at selling, so the more people you meet and ask, "How can I help you?", you begin building a network of new contacts that will get to know you. You can think of it as "I am having fun meeting people that I can help and will help me someday". You can ask the new people you meet, things like "What do you look for in an ideal customer?" Ask them about their business, how have they been doing it, how did they get started, how did they get their current position, etc. Get to know them. Remember, you're developing a relationship, not making a sale – at least not yet.

What better way to operate then to make it your goal to meet new people? You do not suffer any rejection.

> Ask them for help. You could say, "I am just starting out and I am looking for advice on how to grow my business, who would you call on if you were me?"

Most important of all, have FUN! Look forward to who you will meet each day and with wonder about who you might meet. Keep a smile on your face and let the world know you are having fun. See what that kind of enthusiasm will bring you.

Cold call five top prospects each day. Since cold calling has the lowest odds of success, make your targets *outrageous*. Cold call accounts that you only dream about. Remember, your dreams can come true. Why not start here?

> **Tip:**
> "When you cold call, make them BIG, real BIG."

Call at the top (who calls the president anyway?). Cold call only the top prospects in your targeted market. Since the odds aren't great, go for it.

With 25 calls per week on top prospects, even with a 2% return on 1,250 calls annually, that would give you 25 appointments with the top prospects in your market.

Russell Conwell used to say, "There are diamonds in your backyard." Your diamond mine is your customer list. Mine it weekly or monthly depending on how large the list is. Ask your customers "Who do you know who might introduce me to a company I want to do business with or who could you recommend me to?" These diamonds are sitting on the ground, compared to cold calling. With cold calling, you have to dig the mine first. Referrals from your existing customers are like diamonds in a stream. If you have dealt with everyone with integrity and given to each what you want to get, if you have left everyone a little better than you found them in every moment, your customers will gladly help. You will get what you have been giving.

CHAPTER 19: LOVE BEING BETTER THAN YOU WERE YESTERDAY – EVERYDAY

Don't wait for management to review you or don't have regret over you behavior if you are the CEO/Owner

Ask yourself, what did I do today to:

- » Get closer to my goals?
- » Get closer to my income needs?
- » Train my customers?
- » Get more productivity and customers?

Great sales people review themselves constantly! I used to wonder why salespeople who worked for me, waited for me to review them, and quite frankly, I wondered why I needed them.

One of the reasons that someone might want to review themselves daily would be the goal of "Personal Improvement". We all have personal habits that are holding our sales back. Jim Rohn, the powerful motivational speaker and the nation's premier business philosopher, has said the harder he works on himself, the better his business does. Ask your boss for the things he or she would like to see you improve; ask your family and friends as well. Most of the things you will hear, you already knew deep down inside, but until you take inventory, you won't improve. Next, prioritize that list starting with number one.

Ask your prospects what went wrong after a lost sale, or what they liked about your competitor's offering.

Once you've set your sights on your personal improvement, be patient with yourself. Work on one at a time. Visualize yourself doing the new behavior you're looking for.

I can't count the number of times I've heard a salesperson or even sales managers categorize their employees as one type of sales person or another. Does this sound familiar?

He or she is not a;

- Detail orientated person
- Organized person
- Closer
- Opener
- Maintainer

Aren't these the actual things that are holding you back? Be honest. Never accept these things as the "Proverbial You." Remember, you become what you think about. Change them. You can. Think instead "What do I want to become?" and starting with the end in mind, think about what new behaviors would be required to become that type of person and begin to act like you are that person now. Those new behaviors would become your new habits in as soon as 21 days. Do it.

> **Tip:**
> You are what you say you are.

Say this to yourself daily. Tell your boss that you love being better. Make it your focus and the little things will become easier, instead of being **tremendous** annoyances.

People love doing business with people who are good at what they do. So, make it your goal to be better every day. Your customers, boss,

and co-workers will notice and respect you.

All those around you will want to do what they can to help you. They will want to do it well because they know that you do things well.

If you are sloppy, don't be surprised if your support team is sloppy.

If customers recognize that you are haphazard, don't be surprised if they take advantage of this.

But if you work at being the best every day (try it), you'll be amazed at how this affects, in a wonderful positive way, those around you. Try it at home as well. Your family will react positively towards you as well. By loving being better, you'll find each day will be more fun.

Work with passion. All too often we choose jobs that we do not love - that do not fill us with passion. We take our lunch pail and work like "serfs in the kingdom" for our masters.

Tip:
"Love Being Better"

Love what you do -- jobs without passion dry the blood in our veins, make our bones brittle and worse, break our souls. If selling is what you can do with a passion, then do it. If not, find the passion. Eleanor Roosevelt once said, "You must do the one thing that you think you cannot do!" Think about how that might change your life. Just Do It.

My goal each day is to leave everyone and everything a little better than I find them. This helps me be fully present in each moment. I do not have to worry about the future or regret the past if I am fully focused on the present. This is the only moment that we ever have. If I am fully present in every moment, the future takes care of itself. I have my goals and dreams and I am only focused on the moment that I have before me.

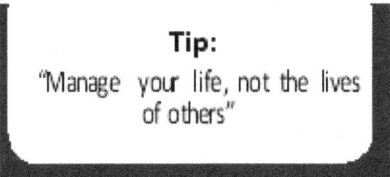

Tip:
"Manage your life, not the lives of others"

When you are always doing your best, you are in "use", honoring your Source, God, the Divine or whatever your Higher Power is for you. You are building your Universal resume. Giving your best means you will get the best in return.

A busy body in sales should be just that, busy with their business and not that of others. I call it the "general manager of the universe syndrome."

Mind your own business. Stay out of the office gossip and politics. I once worked with a group of people who spent more time doing other people's jobs and engaging in office politics. This was a terrible waste of energy and their sales showed it.

Of course, by talking about everyone else, they were deflecting blame from themselves, but the truth was that the result each of these people was getting was lackluster. Let me share with you a quote from Gandhi:

"A true soldier does not argue as he marches, how success is going to be ultimately achieved. But he is confident that if only he plays his humble part well, somehow or other the battle will be won. It is in that spirit that every one of us to know how to do our own part well!"

Make written comments and suggestions every quarter to your management. This is a professional's method of contributing. Stay out of office politics.

Imagine the energy it takes to manage all the affairs of those around you. Some people are "drama addicts." They spend a considerable amount of their time caught up in other people's drama. Jeffrey Gittomer, in his book *The Little Red Book of Selling* says, "The less time you spend in other people's business and other people's drama, the more time you'll have for your own success."

I realized, about 10 years ago or so, that I could have so much
 more time in my life if I spent more time managing my life and less time managing the lives of those around me. People and events were things that I could not control anyway, so why waste the time and energy? I decided to give it up.

From that moment on, I spent most of my energy managing me. Now, mind you, I say most of my energy. I am human and I do catch myself in the drama of others from time to time. I notice it faster and as soon as I do, I get back on track. Many people around me note that I accomplish much and have a lot on my plate. It's not difficult for me to manage more because I am only managing my stuff most of the time. Those same people complain that they do not have enough time. If they gave up their role as "general manager of the universe" they would add enormous amounts of time and energy to their day. What they accomplish in life would increase dramatically. The minute you go in a new direction and make a new choice, new results appear. It's a law of the Universe -- the Universal Law of Cause and Effect.

CHAPTER 20: REMEMBER - "WHAT GOES AROUND, COMES AROUND"

Look in the mirror, wherever you are in your sales career, you are responsible for it. You are just where you should be according to your thoughts and actions. Accept it. Don't beat yourself up over it, but face it. Others are not to blame; the company is not to blame, nor your co-workers, and not your parents - **YOU ARE.** Remember this: "Incompetents invariably make trouble for people other than themselves!" © by Larry McMurtry

Whenever I work with people who are blaming everyone in their company for their lack of performance, I like to hand them a mirror. People who are always blaming others for their lack of success are only deflecting the blame from themselves. So, accept it -- it's yours -- then move on. You are the creator of your life. Warner Erhard once said, "I accuse you of being a circumstance in your life". If you are a circumstance, then you are in "victim" mode. If you believe that things are happening to you, then you are in victim mode.

> **Tip:**
> You are the creator of your life.

Things have not happened to you, you have created these events.

You are attracting the events and people that you need to see, in order to grow. That's why it happens that certain events or people continually show up in our lives.

Until we see it and learn a new behavior, we are destined to repeat the events or meet similar types of people. You cannot grow until you accept the responsibility, but don't linger over it. Instead, learn from your past in fact, laugh. Yes, laugh at your past, (you're not the only one with a past) then write down some goals for personal improvement. Do you think that professional athletes linger long over the missed putt, the crash on the first turn, the strike out, the fumble, the wild pitch? The successful ones certainly do not. Just keep your eyes on where you intend to be, not on where you have been. Use the past as a lesson or sign posts, so that you do not take that same road over and over. Here is a poem that I wrote over ten years ago for people who worked for me (at least that is what I thought, back when I wrote it). I came to realize a few years later that I wrote it for me. I was the biggest obstacle in my life and I had my head in a bad place as you will see.

It can't be me
By Stephen P. Lentini

Lots of people do better than me

I bitch and moan, kick and scream, I am unable to reach my dream.

I work hard, I think I'm smart It's those around me, it's their part.

They're the reason, I've failed to start. They keep me down I know it's true At every turn, it's me they screw.

And so it goes, every day, I get Up and I'm on my way.

Convinced I'm not to blame - it can't be me, what a shame!

Wait, was that a mirror I just passed, no way, can't be, that person had their head up their a_ _!

> **Tip:**
> "Remember, you reap what you sow. What goes around comes around"

"Respect nature and learn from the seasons"

What is the result now of your last springtime? Are you reaping a bountiful harvest? What are you currently harvesting in the direct result of the quality and amount of "seeding" that you did last spring? Did you select the proper soil? Did you neglect to inspect the seeds? Did you take proper care to prepare the ground before planting? Nature provides us with a perfect model to follow and yet we humans think that these same patterns do not apply to our lives. We expect to reap a bountiful harvest even though we rested or procrastinated when we should have been planting. Think about the kind of harvest you want before you plant. Sow lies, reap lies. Sow lack of integrity, reap a lack of integrity in return. Sow procrastination, reap a bleak future. Sow honesty, reap honesty. Sow loyalty and commitment, reap loyalty and commitment in return. The one thing that we forget is that nature returns more than what is sowed by many thousand times over. Just think, from that one tomato seed you sow, the tomato plant returns thousands of seeds. The same is true in our lives. The Law is the Law. Jim Rohn says in his book *The Seasons of Life*, "Faith further provides to us an irrevocable law decreed in heaven which assures that for every disciplined human effort we will receive a multiple reward… for each cup planted, a bushel reaped." Whatever we choose to put into the soil of life will surely return to us multiplied. That is why, if we sow inaction, we reap a future of despair. What are you sowing in your business or on the job? What about at home and with your family and friends? Can you honestly say that you sow love, forgiveness, gratitude and understanding? What would the harvest be from seeds such as these, especially with the guarantee of a multiplied return?

What you expect to harvest begins with the seeds and the discipline of preparing and planting in the spring. It's never too late to begin planting anew. Start now. After planting your seeds of your new future, resist the urge to "rush to the harvest". Humans always want to rush to harvest in their lives. Would you plant an apple tree seed and then stand over it saying "Okay, where are the apples?" No, of course we wouldn't. It sounds ridiculous, and yet that is exactly what we do in our lives. Very often, we expect quick results or riches. We want to "rush to the harvest". Instead, during your winter of planning for your next harvest, write down, in addition to what seeds you will plant, a plan for nurturing the crop. Allow enough time for your seeds to sprout, grow and develop a young crop, and then a bountiful harvest is more likely. Allow time for the full cycle of seasons, one cannot rush nature and that is her message for us as well. Also, allow for bugs and pests, (negative events and people), an early frost, or any bad weather. In this way, you will not be deterred from your plan of a bountiful harvest. Spring is a time for persistence and perseverance.

In my sales training and seminars over the last 22 years, I have often asked my clients, "What would spring look like if the daffodils, crocus and tulips said 'oh, there's too many rocks in the way, the ground is too hard, or it's too cold, I think I'll quit'." Do not quit when it looks like things are difficult. There are tools required to prepare the ground and to plant properly.

Just as the farmer requires the proper tools and equipment to prepare and plant, the tools required for a good planting are a positive attitude, giving what we want to get, action, forgiveness, patience, love, gratitude, opening up, measuring and tracking, visualization, acting as if, speaking as if, change and awareness of choice. All of these things together will bring us a new harvest -- one unlike the past. Without choice and change, we would use all of the other tools to sow, but we would reap the same past harvest over and over. We must be willing to expand and go beyond where we have sown before, with all of the above, for each of the tools mentioned are separate crops as well. Depending on how you use them, you are sowing a future harvest from each of them. Whatever we sow in forgiveness for example, we reap when we require forgiveness ourselves. Whatever we have sown in love, patience or action, we too have reaped. If we work continually to expand where we have gone before, like the Universe is expanding, we will reap a harvest of many new benefits. Jim Rohn says in his book *The Seasons of Life*, "The act of planting during the warm breezes of spring requires that we exert the pain of human discipline and being unwilling to do so assures that in the coming fall, we shall surely experience the greater pain of regret – the difference is that the pain of discipline weighs ounces, and the pain of regret weighs tons. We must either plant during the springtime of our life, or beg from others during the fall."

Prosperity is related to what you are thinking about in every moment.

Your outer world reflects your inner world. Remember what Earl
Nightingale said, "You become what you think about." If your predominant thought pattern is about being frustrated, your outer world will reflect frustration back to you. If there never seems to be enough money, look at what you were taught at home about money. Was lack the predominant pattern at home? "Money doesn't grow on trees." Remember that one? Look also at your giving. You need to look at every level of giv-

ing. Are you generous? Would your family or friends describe you as giving? Are you generous with your money, time, forgiveness, love, consideration, etc.? Get into action, giving more of everything that you have, and give what you want to get. Look at all the areas above, love, time, forgiveness, consideration, appreciation, praise, acknowledgement, etc. Would you like to have more of all of those things? Get into action, giving what you want to get.

Tithing

One of the Universal Laws is "You can't give what you don't have." Research Tithing. All of the most successful people tithe! John D. Rockefeller's first tithe was $9.00. He ended his life having tithed over $500,000,000. And don't forget, he started in the 1800's and died in the early 1900's. What would that be worth in today's dollars? When asked about his wealth, he would say, "GOD gave me my money." If you begin tithing, even if you think you do not have the funds to do it, the universe will support your decision because you must have it to give it. You are "acting as if." Start with giving 10% of what you have left after paying everything, including yourself. The theory of tithing is that you are honoring a higher power. Tithing says that you have faith that you will be taken care of. After all, even the smallest creatures on earth are taken care of, why not you? Money will begin to appear for you. I started tithing 10% of my net pay almost three years ago. During my health challenge, I was out of work for six months. I had over $24,000 come in the mail to me from people who had heard of my circumstances in just over three months. I did not need disability insurance (and I did not have any).

Today I tithe 10% of my net pay, 10% of my training and speaking events, and 10% of my book sales. Each year I add more and more income and I give out more and more. There is always plenty to spare and share. I figure that I did not come here with any money and I will not leave with any, so I must be here to manage it and have fun with it, and I do. Give what you want to get.

CHAPTER 21: MOTIVATE, MOTIVATE, MOTIVATE THOSE AROUND YOU

Read everything pertaining to sales and to personal growth as a way to keep your motivation high. Read about how the Universe works and how successful people have a Higher Power in their life. Read *Think and Grow Rich, and the Universal Laws of Success* by Napoleon Hill. Read *As a Man Thinketh* by James Allen. Read books by Wayne Dyer, Deepak Chopra, Mark Victor Hansen, Jack Canfield and Jim Rohn. Read books on selling, like *The Sales Bible and the Little Red Book of Selling* by Jeffrey Gittomer. Read *Selling is Dead* by Marc T. Miller and Jason M. Sinkovitz.

And read *The Power of a Positive No* by William Ury and *The World's Greatest Salesman* by Og Mandino

Develop your relationship with your Higher Power, as you define it. God, The Universe, The Divine, however you see the energy all around us, see it as a way to understand why you are here, and motivating yourself will be easy. You can leave all the hard stuff to your Higher Power and do what is on your plate to do in each moment. Leave the rest up to Her or Him.

Read biographies about successful people or about anyone you admire --absorb them and consider adding to your own personality, a trait or strategy you found interesting. If it worked for others, why not give it a try? If you will not read, isn't that the same as someone who cannot read? Isn't the long term effect the same? Books on tape, CD, an iPOD, Audible or MP3 are the same thing. Just find a way to do it.

Buy the books. Buy the one day or two day seminars to get incremental changes in your behavior. Invest in reinforcement training that pertains to behavioral and attitude training -- not techniques only. This type of training is usually conducted over a long period of time. They vary from 12 weeks to 3 years or more. If you own or owned a company, or are employed as a salesperson, you are challenged today to motivate your sales support team to help you reach your goals. Teach, train, build, and respect your support staff. Listen to them. Push the cart, don't whip the ox. Help them help you get where you want to go. Include them, perhaps in the success. I've heard many salespeople say, "It's their job. They get paid to support me and it's what I expect." True, but do you think their support team went the extra mile for them. No way. Find a way to make it fun. Find a way for your team to get a win. Everyone loves winning. Sports teams know the objective with each game and they know who won in the end. Come up with something your support team can win daily, weekly, or monthly. Give them a reason to cheer and celebrate the win if they achieve it.

Have integrity. Do what you say. Your employees are watching and will know in an instant if you say one thing and do another.

Don't forget the losses. But review them in a blame proof atmosphere and remind your team that they take the field again tomorrow. A win is only around the corner. Have a crew of committed others to support you.

Acknowledge and praise them. Send them notes of appreciation and thank you's. Ask them what they would like in a gift and send them the gift; whatever it takes to let them know that you care. If people know you care, you can demand more.

CHAPTER 22: DREAM AND BELIEVE IN POSSIBILITIES

That's right. Dream, daydream, picture yourself where it is you want to be. Dream it. Believe it. Do it. Use your imagination machine. Use your imagination power to manifest your deepest desires. Visualize the goal and the rewards of achieving it. Spend some time alone -- at the beach, in the woods, wherever you find peace, -- and see yourself doing what you want.

Imagine yourself with the rewards of dream -- the big boat, the fame, the power, the money, whatever you want -- be there, at your goal, in your dreams. Imagine yourself with the family love and support. Imagine yourself satisfied with what you have. Be grateful. Feel what it feels like to always be grateful. The most successful people in sports visualize the outcome they want.

> **Do it**. Selling will become easier when you see your outcomes first.

To assist your visualizing process, spend some quiet time each day if you can or at least weekly. Create an image book that has pictures, quotes, affirmations, incantations and words that support your goals. Look at it twice daily, once when you first get up and once before you go to sleep. Studies have shown these times to be the most powerful times to impress anything on your subconscious mind. Begin to "act as if" you were already what you wanted to become and act like you already have what you wanted to have.

If satisfaction and fulfillment in life is your number one goal, begin to act as if you were satisfied and fulfilled already. My teacher, Toni Stone says that "Satisfaction is first a decision, feelings follow." She teaches that if one is not satisfied now, then they will never be satisfied later. They will always be satisfied.... when? When this happens or that happens, that is when they will be satisfied. The key is to be satisfied now, so that you will always be in a satisfied state of mind. There is no in between, if you are not satisfied, you will never be satisfied. Make the decision now, be satisfied.

Intention and visualization work together to help us manifest our deepest desires. Get the book, *The Power of Intention* by Wayne Dyer. Use visualization along with intending what you desire daily. Rent the movie "What the Bleep Do We Know and The Secret". Study the Law of Attraction. Your thoughts, words and actions have power. Einstein said that "There is no power greater than the power of imagination." Imagine yourself succeeding, dream dreams beyond where your mortal mind tells you is possible. Have that "BHAG" goal, as Mark Victor Hansen recommends, that "Big Hairy Audacious Goal." Why not? You can imagine anything. Feel what it would feel like to arrive at your goal. See the celebration. All of these steps contribute towards you reaching your goal.

Visualization has great power to bring one quicker to where one wants to go.

Dream on

By Stephen P. Lentini

Dream on, don't quit,

Dreamers seem to never fit.

They're off to lands,
We know not where,

But then again we'll never dare. Believe you must! Is what they say, Soon will come a golden day.

Never ever lose sight of it. Please. Please. Don't ever quit. Keep on dreamin', it's what you must, if you'll ever see what you think just

"I have no patience with people who are always raising difficulties," said Winston Churchill.

Possibilities, on the other hand, are another story. I cannot say for sure, although it's a safe bet that Churchill preferred people who believed in possibilities.

Each occurrence in our life holds a new opportunity, whether it is for personal or monetary growth. By always looking for the possibilities for growth, growth will come. Believe it.

Your imagination knows no limits. Imagine your future.

Napoleon Hill and Ernest Holmes once said that "You would not have the

desire for something if you did not have the ability to bring it forth."

If you feel a desire to achieve something special in your life,

imagine it and feel what it feels like to have already achieved it, and then get on to doing it.

CHAPTER 23: STOP THE WHINING AND START WINNING

I've met and worked with salespeople who whined more than a 6-yearold who wanted that new toy. The time that they spent whining could have been spent calling a new prospect for an appointment. I had no patience for these people because their whining sapped my energy. Stay away from whiners -- they sap your energy. If you are a whiner, stop. Use the energy for winning. Think of all that time you have spent whining, as wasted. You could have been selling. As soon as you catch yourself whining, stop it. Gradually, this stupid habit will disappear and you will see that you have more time for selling and winning.

Your world is an outer picturing of your predominant thought patterns. Negative thinking creates a negative experience. If you don't like your experience of the world, change how the world is experiencing you.

You are the only one in this life that you can control. As you change, things will change. Track your responses to the people and events in your life. Where are you reacting the same way over and over and expecting a different outcome? Step back from those people, prospects, bosses, family, etc. and think about what would be a new response for

you. What would be something new to say or do? When

you do, you will start to see a new life form right before your eyes and the only one who changed was you.

Good selling requires a lot of energy. Great selling requires even more. So guard your energy levels by staying positive, and keeping away from negative people. This includes customers, co-workers, bosses, and spouses – whomever.

If you are working in a negative company, get out. Move on -- there's a big world out there and a life beyond the company you are at. If the company cannot support your efforts, first find a way to support your company. Suggest new ways of doing things. Complain with a request or suggestion. If this does not work, find a new company.

Usually, negative people are unable to change. This is who they are and how they view the world.

Surround yourself with people who see possibilities and let no one put obstacles up between you and your goals. Once you have your goals set, guard your energy. Say it out loud. Practice saying "Sorry – believing it cannot happen or that we are blocked in any way from succeeding does not work for me." "Can we focus on what would work or how to get around this temporary obstacle?"

Tip: Remind yourself frequently

"Your energy is one of your most Important assets"

You will find yourself identifying time and

energy-draining people

and customers and avoiding them

Selling will be a lot easier and more fun.

I know it's an old cliché but - refuse to let negative

thoughts into your mind. Try picturing a door in your mind and when a negative thought

enters, close the door, say "Thank you for sharing" and close the door.

Use affirmations! Anything that follows the words "I am" is an affirmation. You are the programmer of your mind. Listen to the words you are currently using in your everyday conversations. You will be amazed to hear some of the things that you are programming. Be clear, direct and concise in your words, and amazing things will follow. Think about all the negative events in your life? Did you think about them casually before they happened? Did you ever casually wish for something that appeared later in your life?

When you can see that you have created all the negative events in your life, you will see your own power to create. You will see just how powerful you are. Be intentional with your thoughts and words. Have them match what you long for. Whatever is your deepest longing, go for it. Eleanor Roosevelt once said, "You must do what you think you cannot do!" Be intentional with your thinking and speaking. Remember, you have created your world up until now without disciplined thinking or a focused effort.

Listen carefully to what you speak about and think about. You are the creator of your circumstances. You are not at the effect of your circumstances. You are a powerful co-creator of your world. I say co-creator because I believe in a higher power in my life. I think about the fact that we live in a galaxy, in a Universe. I believe that I can tap into that power to create what I deeply desire. You can too. I have a coach and the support of others to help me stay on track. Disciplined and focused. I am achieving my deepest desires. As a spiritual salesperson, you can prove the power you have to create by following the ideas in this book and experiment. Prove these concepts to yourself. We do afterall, live in a miracle, a Universe. Look up the Neville Goddard story and try his "Mind-Movie" visualization practice and you will be amazed at what you manifest in your life. The Life you have only dreamed of!

CHAPTER 24: WE DO LIVE IN A GALAXY, IN A UNIVERSE

Take some quiet time each day, preferably 6am and 6pm, to reflect on the fact that we live in a Galaxy, in a Universe. During my health challenge, I had a moment in intensive care that truly changed the rest of my life. I was in the hospital for a little over four days, since Wednesday, and on Monday afternoon my friend Warren and my significant other, Janice, were visiting me. I remember seeing Janice and Warren one second, being in the hospital room with them, and the next second I was one with everything and nothing, it was just a knowing, pure consciousness... no body and "I" was there..." In the next second, my life review ... only the good I had done, the lives I had touched flashed before me. Next I was asked, very gently, very lovingly, "Stay or go?" That was it, nothing else. I remember in that moment feeling very peaceful and thinking "Well, I have touched a lot of lives. Thy will be done." I surrendered my life to the will of the Universe, God or the Divine Consciousness. In that next second, I was back in the hospital room. When I was comfortable with sharing that story some weeks later with Warren and Janice, Warren mentioned that "It was Monday, November 18th at around 2pm." "Your vitals has crashed and the nurses and doctors came rushing in to intensive care and said to us out out, this is it call his family."

I am certain that one of the reasons that I came back is to share this story that we are always safe, connected to the Divine, the Universe, and living a miracle, as well as living in a miracle, in every moment. And that we have nothing to fear. To encourage people to live from the level of their soul and not the material world.

I have since remembered, not perfectly mind you, to surrender when I think that things are out of control. That I have nothing to fear since I have faced death, and that even in death, we have nothing to fear. We are safe, always and in every moment. At the moment of my death, there was no mention of anything I had achieved or failed to achieve. There was no mention of anything that I had acquired, nothing material at all. The only mention was of the people I had touched. The good I had done.

How many of us live working hard to achieve, and never stop to really be with and touch the people in our lives? How many of us really care, in each moment, of the other person in front of us? How many of us are only thinking of a quota or a promotion or the praise and accolades we will receive if we can "just close this customer?"

Take the time to really be with your customers and prospects. Really feel what you are feeling and work to help your customers and prospects find the best solution for them, even if it is not you. You get what you give and the Universe will reward you.

When you look up in the sky at night, we too are just one of those little twinkling stars. Physicists and astronomers, with the help of the Hubble telescope, confirm now that just in our galaxy alone there are over 200 billion suns with planets that circle them. That's in our galaxy alone! We live in a miracle. Take time each day to reflect on that and remember to bring miracle thinking with you in each moment. The Universe is infinite, so bring some infinite possibility thinking with you as well. Imagine the energy that someone who thinks this way brings to every moment.

I salute the Divine in each person, silently, and send them my blessings as a gift. This helps me to detach from the outcome and to remember that I do live in a Galaxy, in a Universe.

Don't worry about your quotas. Keep making sales calls, looking to help people buy, and be fully present with them, intending to help them, and you will be successful. I have been. Deepak Chopra, says in his book *Power, Freedom and Grace*, "As you elevate your attention from the world of the humdrum and trivial to the world of the magical and miraculous, your life becomes magical and miraculous. Your attention is spontaneously alert to the fact that life itself is a miracle. And the more you put your attention on miracles, the more you become the conscious creator of miracles"

I urge you to bring your attention up to the level of the Divine -- the miraculous in every moment -- even in those moments when someone or something is bothersome, difficult or even tragic. We cannot always see the miracle immediately or the reason for these difficult moments, and usually some time later, we can see why they happened or how they contributed immensely to our growth, to our lives.

Try it for two or three years and see if you live a more joyful, successful, satisfied life.

The Divine is always with us. It has no religion, no sex, no race, it is pure consciousness. Rest assured that as a spiritual salesperson, you are on a miraculous journey with the Divine. All and everyone are the Divine nudging you along on your way. What you think is a bump in the road is the Divine tweaking you... moving you towards the right path.

Some people and events really bugs us and especially those events... they are the Divine making us aware of what needs changing. Perhaps we have similar qualities of those who bugs us and they are in our life to show us we have those same traits. Some events are necessary ingredients to get us to the life we dream of. A great prayer is "God, you promised me the desires of my heart, in fact, you put them there so I know this person or event that feels negative or hurts is actually a blessing in disguise. Even though I can not see it yet, I know this is a blessing and moving me to the dream, thank you God."

Thank you is the highest form of pray. Make the Divine your best friend and do good in this world. Live with passion and love what you do until you can do what you love. Trust that God, the Goddess, the Divine is working in every moment of your life and relax and let go knowing this is so.

Reach out to me anytime, I am grateful that you purchased this book. It's a wink from the Divine.

Thank you.

Steve

Steve Lentini is an author, teacher, trainer and dynamic Public Speaker on the Universal Laws of Success, Sales and Sales Management, Leadership and Quality Rated Customer Service.

With more than 40 years of sales management experience, Stephen P. Lentini is the CEO of Lentini Sales Leadership
and the Director of The Prosperity Institute, a business consulting and training company in Staten Island, NY.

He writes, teaches and trains on a variety of sales and management topics for audiences nationwide. He is a published author with the following books on Kindle and Amazon;

Sales Success for Rookie, How to Succeed at Sales Right From the Start,

Sales Success for Veteran Sales People, How to Gain a Strategic Edge and Close More Sales, Wake up, Jump into Your Life and Sales Success for the Spiritual Salesperson, How to Sell without Losing your Soul.

He has sold, owned businesses, managed sales people, consulted, coached, and trained for over 45 years.

He is currently writing, teaching and developing other books.

Steve can be reached at 917-805-1088 or email at steve@stevelentini.com

and on his website, www.stevelentini.com are free eBooks on other of his favorite topics